Gender, Time, and Reduced Work

SUNY Series in
THE SOCIOLOGY OF WORK

Richard H. Hall, Editor

Gender, Time, and Reduced Work

Cynthia Negrey

STATE UNIVERSITY OF NEW YORK PRESS

HD
5110.2
U5
N44
1993

Production by Ruth Fisher
Marketing by Bernadette LaManna

Published by
State University of New York Press, Albany

For information, address State University of New York
Press, State University Plaza, Albany, NY 12246

Library of Congress Cataloging-in-Publication Data

Negrey, Cynthia, 1953–
    Gender, time, and reduced work / Cynthia Negrey.
      p. cm. — (SUNY series in the sociology of work)
    Includes bibliographical references and index.
    ISBN 0–7914–1407–8 (hb : acid-free) — ISBN 0–7914–1408–6 (pb :
acid-free)
    1. Part-time employment—United States. 2. Work sharing—United
States. 3. Temporary employment—United States. 4. Sexual division
of labor—United States. 5. Work and family—United States.
I. Title. II. Series.
HD5110.2.U5N44   1993
331.4'0973—dc20
                                             92–11955
                                               CIP

10 9 8 7 6 5 4 3 2 1

"A society that gives to one class all the opportunities for leisure and to another all the burdens of work dooms both classes to spiritual sterility."

—Lewis Mumford

Contents

List of Tables

Preface

I began this project in the wake of the twin recessions of 1979–1982. As a native of the nation's industrial heartland, I watched mighty production centers become ghost towns and steel turn to rust. During that economic debacle I often pondered work-time reduction as what seemed to me to be a pragmatic strategy for alleviating unemployment. My curiosity about such a public policy led me to explore the literature on work-time reduction, both the renewed calls for work-time reduction that appeared in the early 1980s and the historical literature on working hours legislation and previous efforts to reduce work time. At the same time that I was studying this literature and becoming aware of a largely invisible movement to reduce work time in the United States, I was also aware of increasing part-time and temporary employment. On the one hand, there were those promoting work-time reduction as if it were something that had not yet occurred at the same time that some people in the society were already experiencing work-time reduction on a voluntary or involuntary basis. I asked myself how I could make sense of these seeming contradictions.

At first I was inclined to ignore these two faces of work-time reduction. I had heard of an organization in Flint, Michigan, called the Center for New Work. Individuals affiliated with that center were hoping to find a UAW local willing to experiment with a six months on/six months off employment scheme. Under this arrangement, half of a plant's work force would work full-time for six months while the other half would be off. At the conclusion of the six month period, the two halves of the work force would switch places. During the time that workers were off, they could participate in programs sponsored by the Center for New Work to learn constructive ways of using their time off. I desperately wanted to study this experiment in work-time alternatives, but the longer I waited the more I realized the experiment was not going to happen. Despite Flint's dire economic straits, the idea was apparently just too progressive. But my curiosity about work-time issues lingered. That is when I turned my focus to "already existing" forms of reduced work. I pieced together the comparative analysis that became this book in an effort to understand the plusses and minuses of work-time reduction and the social forces giving rise to varied forms of reduced work in the closing decades of the twentieth century.

Chapter one sets the context for understanding reduced work. In addition to defining the concept, I examine the recent and ongoing structural changes in the U.S. economy that have motivated scholars, public policy officials, and workers to advocate work-time reduction. I also discuss the economic and social forces that have led to recent increases in conventional part-time and temporary employment, or "market forms" of reduced work, and those forces that have led to experiments with "negotiated forms" of reduced work, such as job sharing and work sharing. Because many advocates of work-time reduction argue that it enhances personal autonomy, I explore those theoretical claims in chapter one as well.

Chapter two is a discussion of the body of scholarship that informs and is informed by my analysis of reduced work, particularly the literature on segmented labor markets, work hours and work schedules, and the gender division of labor in the household. Then begins my empirical analysis of reduced work and personal autonomy. Chapter three explains the procedures of data collection and analysis that are the foundation for this book. It also profiles the characteristics of the workers I interviewed in each of the four categories of reduced work, highlighting important demographic differences. Chapter four focuses on the conventional part-time workers, first introducing part-time employment in general terms, then examining the part-time workers I interviewed for their reasons for working part-time, their work schedules, and how part-time employment affects their use of time off the job and their quality of life more generally. In chapter five I apply the same logic to an examination of temporary employment. In chapter six I turn to a focused analysis of job sharing; what it is, how it differs from more conventional part-time employment, why people share jobs, work schedules among those job sharers I interviewed, and how they use their time off the job. The work sharers are discussed in chapter seven. There I explain work sharing as an idea and employment practice, then I discuss why my informants entered into the work-sharing scheme at their place of employment and how they use their time off the job. The concluding chapter, chapter eight, draws together insights from a comparative analysis of the four types of reduced work, returns to the theoretical appraisal of reduced work outlined in chapter one, and raises practical issues for public debate regarding current forms of reduced work.

Acknowledgments

I revel in the creative challenge that is intellectual work, but at times my confidence falters as I face new hurdles in a seemingly daunting task. Throughout the years that I worked on this project, many individuals offered support, encouragement, and practical advice that helped me better organize my thoughts, sharpen my focus, and articulate key concepts. I want to take this occasion to thank them.

First and foremost, I want to extend my heartfelt appreciation to those persons who volunteered to be interviewed for this study and who assisted in the recruitment of volunteers. While they must remain nameless here, without them this project most certainly could not have been completed.

This book originated as a dissertation completed in the sociology department at Michigan State University. There, Richard Child Hill, William Faunce, Ruth Simms Hamilton, Kevin Kelly, and Katherine O'Sullivan See provided guidance in defining and completing the research that became the basis for my dissertation and ultimately this book. Stephen Esquith helped me identify and articulate the duality of market and negotiated forms of reduced work. Frithjof Bergmann of the University of Michigan affirmed that there was indeed a larger audience for scholarship on work-time issues. Members of my dissertation support group were important intellectual and social companions when this project was in that early stage of development: Nancy Buffenbarger, Ginger Macheski, Mary McCormack, Virginia Powell, Delores Wunder, JoAnn Belknap, Mary Roberson, Marion McCoy, Jo Dohoney, Ruth Harris, Vandana Kohli, and Georgann Lenhart. Several of these individuals have continued to offer encouragement and support since my departure from East Lansing.

I am grateful to Carmen Sirianni for encouraging me to publish this research in book form; his own scholarship on the political economy of working time blazes a theoretical trail that I like to believe my work follows. Without the patient guidance and unyielding support of my editor at SUNY, Rosalie Robertson, however, this project would not have matured to its current form. Whether she knew it or not, she always spoke the right words at the right time to buoy my confidence and keep me motivated. I also want to thank Richard Hall, the series editor, for his confidence in this project and the anonymous reviewers, whose comments were most instrumental in giving this book its final shape. Irene Padavic offered comments on a paper that forced me to think more critically about my conclusions here.

Several friends in Louisville and elsewhere—Mark Austin, Susan Bennett, Melissa Evans-Andris, Sally Gello, Michael Giordano, Elayne Jacoby, Joe Jacoby, Frances Purifoy, Ron Vogel, Allen Whitt, and Cynthia Woolever—were participants in an ongoing conversation as I thought out loud to transform my dissertation into this book. Without them, it would have been a much lonelier process. I also want to thank the Department of Sociology at the University of Louisville, and department chair Thomas Keil in particular, for giving me a one-course reduction in my teaching load during the fall semester 1991 which permitted me to complete the final manuscript.

Finally, I want to thank my parents, George and Phyllis Negrey, for supporting my ambitions. It was as a youth in their home that I first pondered the liberatory promise of reduced work. That early thinking may have been naive, and I am now more circumspect for having completed the research for this book. But I still hold out hope that the reduction and control of working time can be steps toward a more just society.

Chapter One

The Best of Both Worlds?

Today increasing numbers of workers in the United States are employed less than full-time, some by personal choice, others by economic fiat. The form of less-than-full-time employment, or reduced work, may vary as may the type of occupation and the industry within which a less-than-full-time worker is employed. Certain types of reduced work, such as conventional part-time employment and temporary employment, are concentrated among women who work in sales and clerical jobs. Many part-time jobs are in the retail trade and services industries. Other types of less-than-full-time employment, such as job sharing, are concentrated among professionals and clerical workers, many of whom are employed in large, bureaucratic organizations in the private and public sectors. The vast majority of job sharers are women, most seeking to better integrate wage work with household and child care responsibilities. Work sharing is concentrated among production workers in manufacturing and construction, thus many work sharers are men. The form of reduced work, the type of occupation, and the industry in which a worker is employed influence his or her income, work schedule, and use of time off the job. In a global sense, the form of reduced work (as it intersects occupation and industry) influences a worker's quality of life, particularly through his or her sense of personal autonomy in terms of providing adequately for self and others and the ability to use time off the job in ways the individual desires.

Gender cuts across reduced work at both the macro and micro levels of analysis. Reduced work occurs in the context of a larger sex/gender system.[1] In this sense reduced work's various forms are in part a product of the different ways gendered labor is used in our economy. Consequently, reduced work tends to reinforce unequal

1

gender relations rather than challenge them. While the type of reduced work, in turn, influences individuals' income, work schedules, and use of time off the job, income in particular must be understood within the larger context of the sex/gender system as it intersects the market economy: men and women tend to be remunerated differentially and unequally because their occupations tend to be sex-segregated. Use of time off the job and quality of life more generally are products of the structural relations outlined here, but the use of time off the job in particular is also influenced by the gender, here at a psychological level, of the individual selecting activities to pursue.

Consider the following examples. Jane Forrester[2] is employed twenty hours a week as a paralegal in a short-time arrangement she negotiated with the attorneys with whom she has worked for fourteen years. The law firm is fairly progressive, and the partners have often expressed their willingness to be flexible in scheduling staff work hours. The thirty-six-year-old mother of two elementary school-age children, Jane wanted to devote less time to her wage-paying job and more time to her family and other interests. Her full-time job paid thirty thousand dollars annually; she was reluctant to take a 50 percent cut in salary, but she and her husband agreed that they could afford it. Jane is secure in the knowledge that she can probably return to full-time hours whenever she wants to do so, or if she needs to do so. When she began the short-time arrangement, she was uncertain how long she would sustain it. In her mind it was indefinite unless it became untenable.

Jane negotiated her work schedule with the attorneys. Although they occasionally face deadline pressure, there are enough other paralegals on staff that Jane is not indispensable. She is a valued employee however, so they do not want to lose her. Jane is something of a morning person so she prefers a work schedule of 9:00 AM to 1:00 PM Monday through Friday. She can get to the office by nine easily after sending her children off to school, and she still has time in the morning for a quick, quiet breakfast after everyone else has left the house. At the office she is at her best because she feels fresh. By one o'clock, however, she often starts to drag and is eager for a change of pace. She leaves the office, grabs a quick lunch on her way home or at home, then does household chores or runs errands. Sometimes she uses the afternoon to prepare a special meal for her family. Other times, she takes advantage of a free afternoon to go swimming at a local community center. She always plans to be at home by four o'clock, however, when her children return from school. Her husband usually arrives home by six o'clock, and soon after the family always sits down to dinner together.

Jane spends most evenings at home with her family, watching television with them or perhaps going off to another room to read or sew or listen to music, but one evening a week, sometimes two if she is working on a special project, she attends meetings of her favorite political group to keep abreast of events, help raise funds, and the like. On those evenings, she scurries from the dinner table and leaves her husband in charge of cleaning up and supervising the children.

What Jane likes most about her lifestyle is its variety. "Variety is the spice of life," she often says. She is employed at a job she loves, but it does not consume her life. She has a balance of employment, family life, community service, recreation, and solitude. She achieves this balance because she is not employed at a full-time job and because she has a lot of control over the scheduling of her varied activities. Within the constraints of her time at the office, her children's school hours, her husband's work schedule, and the time of her political meetings, Jane manages to cover all the bases. Her broad interests are satisfied because she has time to pursue varied activities. She is aware, however, that her lifestyle is subsidized by her husband's income. If she were a single parent, she could not afford to raise her children on fifteen thousand dollars a year, at least at the standard to which they have become accustomed. She would have to return to full-time employment and might have to give up some of her recreational activities and community service, at least until her children were old enough to leave without adult supervision, unless she took them along or found substitute care.

Alice Francone also works short hours, by conventional standards, but because her hours are irregular and not subject to her control, and because her job pays poorly, she is unable to achieve the sense of balance and autonomy that Jane Forrester has created. Alice has worked as a sales clerk in a retail store for less than a year. She took this job when she and her husband separated, after dropping out of the paid work force for eight years while she raised their young son. Alice panicked when she and her husband separated, anticipating that she might have a difficult time finding a job with her limited employment experience. The offer of the clerk's job came quickly. She accepted it so she would "have something," but she has continued to look for a better job although without much success. She lives in a community where the economic base is shrinking and where few jobs are available. She considers moving, but she is reluctant to take her son farther away from his father, at least for now.

Alice's work schedule varies considerably from week to week. She has requested that she only be scheduled during the hours her son is at school or on weekends when her son can go to his father's apartment. Her supervisor, a single parent herself, has accommodated Alice as much as possible. Alice is usually scheduled to work from twenty to twenty-four hours each week. She is grateful for any hours her employer can give her, and she is secure in the knowledge that she will work at least twenty hours each week. Some weeks she is scheduled four hours a day, five days a week, during the week. Other weeks she might work a four-hour day sandwiched between two eight-hour days, or an eight-hour day sandwiched between several four-hour days. The weekends are unpredictable, too. She might work four hours on both Saturday and Sunday, or eight hours one day, or not at all on the weekend. Her schedule varies according to anticipated sales volume and the availability and scheduling of more senior clerks in her department. Some weeks she works twenty-four hours if the company anticipates a "big week" or if one of the other clerks needs time off or is on vacation.

The irregularity and uncertainty of her work schedule annoy Alice, but she is powerless to alter the situation short of finding another job. Perhaps the greatest annoyance is that she cannot get more hours. Her job pays barely above the minimum wage, and, at twenty or twenty-four hours a week, she just does not make enough money to support herself and her son. She receives child support and an allowance from her husband, and that income helps a lot, but the allowance will only persist a year or two after their divorce is final and the child support payments probably will not keep up with inflation. Alice very much wants to be financially self-supporting, but, from her vantage point now, that seems an impossible goal to achieve. For the time being, she is among the working poor.

Alice spends much of her time off the job doing household tasks and "puttering." She has little discretionary income so she does not even stroll through a nearby shopping mall because she does not want to tempt herself to buy things she really does not need. Occasionally she takes her son to a movie; they always go to second-run showings at a theatre that only charges one dollar for admission. Sometimes she takes him out to eat, to inexpensive family restaurants, but she cannot afford to do that often. For very special occasions, she asks her husband for some extra money, being careful to say it is for their son and not her, but he resents her requests if they are too frequent.

Alice regularly reads the classified ads in the local newspaper hoping to find her dream job. "It's frustrating," she says, "because in months of looking it is just not there." When she does find jobs to apply for, she becomes anxious about the prospect of interviews. "How can I schedule them when I don't know from week to week what my work schedule will be at the store?" she asks plaintively. Her supervisor knows she is looking for a better job and seems willing to work with Alice by being flexible about her schedule, but Alice feels she is walking a thin line. She does not want her supervisor to think she is taking advantage, nor does she want to risk losing hours. She needs all the hours she can get! She wonders if she might need to take a second part-time job, but she is uncertain how she could arrange that job around her irregular schedule at the store and her son's school hours.

Alice has many interests that are unsatisfied. She adores listening to music, but she cannot afford to buy a good sound system. She has a small cassette player that her husband had purchased for her some years ago and a small collection of tapes that she listens to, and, of course, she listens to the radio. "But why do I need a better sound system," she says, "when I can't afford to buy CDs and tapes?" She occasionally takes an hour to work out in her living room in front of an exercise video or sit down and read a book that she has borrowed from the local public library. Her recreational activities all cost very little and can be taken up rather spontaneously. Because her time is so fragmented, she cannot plan many activities. Community service is out of the question. "I can't tell when I'm coming or going," she complains.

The examples of Jane Forrester and Alice Francone illustrate the positive and negative aspects of reduced work for women. Sometimes reduced work facilitates a greater sense of balance and personal autonomy, other times it creates obstacles to achieving such a sense of well being. But these examples also raise several questions of theoretical interest: In what ways does the experience of reduced work differ for men? Would men be in the same types of jobs or different jobs? Would their pay be the same? More? Less? Are men more likely to be concentrated in certain types of reduced work than others? Are they concentrated in different types of reduced work by comparison to women? How would men use their time off the job? Would they find reduced work satisfying or distressing?

Other significant theoretical questions have less to do with gender and more to do with the nature of reduced work per se. The example of Jane Forrester refers to a situation something like job sharing (although she does not share a full-time position with a coworker) because she negotiated her short-time arrangement with her employer. Alice Francone's case, however, is a more conventional form of part-time employment. What difference would it make if these women were temporary employees or in work-sharing arrangements? As women, are they even likely to be in a work-sharing arrangement?

What do different types of reduced work imply for the temporal rhythm of life? Are some types of reduced work likely to be more satisfying than others?

Variations in the experience of reduced work are important to explore in an era when work-time reduction is occurring through market forces. As more and more people work part-time or as temporaries, they may find themselves in situations like Alice Francone's. Their experiences raise significant theoretical and political questions regarding the nature of the society unfolding now. To what extent are individuals marginalized by reduced work? Simultaneously, quasi-utopian visionaries advocate generalized work-time reduction to solve social problems resulting from structural transformations of the economy, such as worker displacement and unemployment, and the increased labor force participation of women, such as child care. Others advocate work-time flexibility to ease the pressures on working parents and to promote more satisfying personal lives by breaking the education-work-retirement lockstep.[3] But are some types of reduced work better than others for solving these sorts of social problems? Is reduced work really a solution to these social problems? This book explores such questions. It encourages advocates of work-time reduction and flexibility to look carefully at the current experience of reduced work, broadly defined, to uncover its promise and limits for individuals' quality of life.

A Comment on Terminology

Before proceeding further, I want to pause to explain my use of the concepts of reduced work and time off the job. Neither concept is entirely satisfactory, but they most closely approximate the ideas I want to convey in this book.

Reduced work is used as an umbrella term to encompass all of the types of less-than-full-time employment I explore: part-time employment, temporary employment, job sharing, and work sharing. It is intended to be broader in scope than the more common concepts of, for example, part-time employment or contingent work. Part-time employment is not entirely accurate in this context since temporary employment may involve full or part-time hours and since the type of work sharing I explore is more like a sabbatical than part-time work. *Contingent work* customarily encompasses part-time and temporary employment, but it is not broad enough nor is it accurate to extend it to include job sharing and work sharing. I considered *short-hours* as an alternative to reduced work, but I rejected it because temporary employment can involve full-time weeks and work sharing does not always take the form of shortened workweeks. Because the notion of short-hours tends to be associated with short workweeks (due to the labeling of efforts to reduce the workweek at different points in history as short-hours movements), it does not precise.y fit the other examples of less-than-full-time employment that I explore here.

Reduced work is broad enough to encompass the varied forms of less-than-full-time employment I studied because it is not necessarily equated with short workweeks. While it includes them, the concept can also be extended to include temporary employment and the sabbatical-like work sharing with which I am concerned. Reduced work can include forms of work-time reduction over the course of the week, the month, the year, or the lifetime. The point is that employment is less than normative full-time, year-round employment. *Work-time reduction* is synonymous with reduced work, and I use it periodically throughout the book as an alternative to reduced work, but it is a cumbersome term to use regularly. I use *short time* similarly.

Yet another problem remains. The term reduced work falls into a sexist trap. Technically, reduced work refers to hours of paid employment, not the unpaid work that individuals may perform after hours. The term is misleading in that reduced work suggests a reduction of work. In actuality, it refers to reduction of one type of work, paid work. It does not incorporate unpaid work. Which leads me to why I prefer the phrase *time off the job* to the more standard non-work time. The concept of non-work time also falls into a sexist trap. It assumes that no work is performed during the time an individual is away from his or her wage-paying job. This is a patently false assumption, particularly when we consider the many hours of household work and child care put in by most women and some men. To avoid the trap that all work is paid and unpaid activities are something other than work (despite falling into this trap with the term reduced work), I use the concept of time off the job to refer to the time and accompanying activities of individuals when they are not at their wage-paying job.

A Context for Understanding Reduced Work

Reduced work at this time in history must be understood within the larger context of post-industrial society and the sex/gender system. The transition from a manufacturing-based to a service-based economy has ramifications for the gender division of labor, both outside and inside the home. And the gender division of labor inside the home influences women's and men's selection of jobs. This sex/gender system contributes to the development of sex-segregated occupations which have implications, in particular, for women's and men's earnings.

Post-Industrialism and Reduced Work

In the late 1970s and early 1980s the advanced capitalist nations, specifically Western European nations and the United States, experienced economic crises the depths of which had not been reached since the Great Depression of the 1930s. While the recent crises seem to have had some cyclical dimensions, the overriding cause lies in the structural transformation of these economies, specifically the shift from manufacturing to services, and the domestic and global relocation of capital. Unskilled production jobs are increasingly located in Third World countries where wages are low and unions are weak or nonexistent. International competition in several manufacturing industries has contributed to the recentering of capital, and communities whose economies are historically rooted in basic manufacturing suffer the consequences of deindustrialization.[4] At the same time, service-type jobs are expanding at a fast rate, and many of these jobs are extensions of the kind of work women do in the home. As service jobs have increased as a percentage of all jobs, women's participation in the paid labor force has increased simultaneously.[5]

Against the backdrop of these turbulent economic conditions, some political leaders, workers, and intellectuals have called for work-time reduction to redistribute the available wage work. In 1978, for example, U.S. Representative John Conyers (D-Michigan) proposed amendments to the Fair Labor Standards Act to reduce the standard workweek from forty to thirty-five hours by 1983, increase premium pay for overtime, and prohibit mandatory overtime. His efforts were unsuccessful; the legislation never progressed beyond committee hearings.[6] Since the 1960s, the AFL-CIO has officially supported reduction of the workweek to thirty-five hours, and more recently International Union of Electrical Workers (IUE) Vice President Peter DiCicco argued for a reduced workweek as the only humane alternative to large-scale labor displacement associated with advances in production technology.[7] The distinguished liberal economist, Lester Thurow, has also advocated a reduction in the workweek.[8]

Workers in several Western European countries have agitated for reductions in working time without loss of pay. Some one million

Dutch workers went to thirty-six-hour weeks in 1984, and the West German metalworkers won a 38.5-hour workweek after a lengthy, bitter strike the same year.[9] One West German company, Beck-Felmeier, a department store in Munich, has even experimented with *flexiyears*, a plan under which employees choose how many hours they want to work in the following twelve months. Workers negotiate with their supervisor to determine the scheduling of those work hours.[10]

Paradoxically, at the same time that appeals for work-time reduction have appeared on the political agenda in numerous advanced capitalist nations, work-time reduction in a sense is taking place. In the United States, for example, there were dramatic increases in part-time and temporary employment during the 1980s. These trends, which will be explored further in chapters four and five, are expressions of the increase in service employment *and* the efforts of corporations to restructure in their quest for renewed profitablility. These market forms of reduced work coexist with negotiated forms, such as job sharing and work sharing. Job sharing, in particular, has evolved as an accommodation made by employed mothers, although it is not exclusively a strategy for merging paid employment with the care of young children. Work sharing, which takes various forms, is a state-organized and/or labor-management-negotiated accommodation to job shortage. These negotiated forms of reduced work will be explored further in chapters six and seven.

Work-time reduction may have lost all political relevance in recent years, considering that the advanced capitalist nations have recovered, to varying degrees, from the economic crises of the early 1980s. Until the current recession, in which the official U.S. unemployment rate has crept upward, the national unemployment rate had dropped to under six percent, and political officials boasted about the longevity of economic recovery. Critics, of course, such as 1988 Democratic vice presidential candidate Lloyd Bentsen, noted the "swiss cheese" nature of this recovery—uneven economic growth that had left parts of the country behind, continuing to struggle with economic decline and uncertainty. What the comparatively low unemployment rate also masked were the increase in part-time and temporary jobs and the increase in the proportion of the labor force involuntarily employed part-time.

Given the structural transformation of the advanced capitalist economies and the continuing participation of employed parents in the paid labor force, it appears that less-than-full-time employment will be a permanent feature of post-industrial society. What is the nature of various forms of reduced work that exist today, and what do they portend for individuals' sense of personal autonomy and quality of life? It is this question that this book addresses.

Occupational Sex Segregation and Reduced Work

The sex/gender system and reduced work are mutually interactive. Jobs are sex-segregated, with women concentrated in clerical, service, and professional occupations and men concentrated in labor, professional, and managerial occupations.[11] Women are 80 percent of clerical workers, 60 percent of service workers, 45 percent of professional and technical workers, 45 percent of sales workers, 28 percent of managerial and administrative workers, 12 percent of nonfarm laborers, and 6 percent of craft workers.[12] As my research will reveal, the different types of reduced work occur with greater or less frequency in different occupational categories and different industrial sectors, and those who work less than full-time are more often women than men. This occurs because women are concentrated in the kinds of jobs where less-than-full-time employment is concentrated. It also occurs because many women actively seek less-than-full-time employment to balance paid employment and family responsibilities. In manufacturing production jobs, however, women tend to be underrepresented. Despite that, they are disproportionately represented among work sharers.[13] To the extent that work sharing is an accommodation to job shortage and differentially affects workers with low seniority, women appear disproportionately among the ranks of work sharers. The work sharers I spoke with for this book, however, are exceptional in that regard. They were high-seniority production workers who volunteered for temporary layoff under an inverse seniority layoff scheme. Because they were high-seniority workers in manufacturing, the work sharers in this book are predominantly men.

Reduced Work, Personal Autonomy, and Quality of Life

Advocates of work-time reduction have argued that reduced work hours would have several social and personal benefits. In addition to redistributing the available wage work and reducing joblessness, reduced work hours could be a factor in energy conservation (fewer trips to and from the job would reduce gasoline consumption) and could engender a more egalitarian division of labor between women and men by providing more time, especially for men, for child care and household work.[14] Most important for my purposes, reduced work could provide greater flexibility in juggling wage work and household responsibilities or other activities and could expand opportunities for education, recreation, and community service.

Based on her survey of job sharers, Gretl Meier reports that the greatest reward of job sharing is the opportunity to balance paid employment with time off the job. She notes,

> Work is central in the lives of job sharers, but not the sole criterion for identity. With one or two exceptions—those who would have preferred full-time jobs—the 238 individuals surveyed see this sense of balance as a result of having the ability to allocate their own time between work and other activities: time for family, children, other interests, time to "gain perspective," "to be refreshed," "time to take a deep breath and know yourself again".…
>
> "I'd be a basket case if I had to work full-time; I'd also be a basket case if I didn't work at all," is a typical statement. Comments from almost every survey questionnaire express the satisfaction, the feeling of relief at having achieved a better sense of balance. "I am better at work, better at home; I can look forward to both because when I come to work I know I still have time for other things, whereas working 40 hours at the same job can become a drag, no matter how much you like the job."[15]

This heightened sense of balance is indicative of the relationship between job sharing and personal autonomy. Time for family, children, and other interests is crucial for those whose identities are distributed across employment and off-the-job activities. Involvement in off-the-job activities is an important dimension of self-expression, and greedy jobs—those that force workers to limit involvement in off-the-job activities—become a source of resentment. On the other hand, because we live in a culture that prizes paid employment and defines employment as a central component of identity, those who forgo employment in favor of other activities lose a measure of social status. Job sharing permits individuals to maintain social status that is derived from employment and allows for expression of those aspects of self that are not identified with employment. If job sharers control their work schedules, which was the case for most of the job sharers I interviewed, their sense of autonomy and control over their lives is further enhanced. Their lives are not dominated by temporal regimes imposed by an employer.

The sense of autonomy derived from control of the work schedule can develop in organizations that permit flexitime. Under flex-itime, workers are permitted to adjust their starting and leaving times to their needs so long as they are on the job for certain core hours. If the job is full-time, however, the worker may still believe that he or she has insufficient time off the job to satisfy non-job-related needs and interests.

Desires for schedule control and work-time reduction are expres-sions of the complexity of life in post-industrial society in the closing decades of the twentieth century. Like the abundance of products that compete for the consumer's dollar, a myriad of activities compete for the individual's time. This surplus of possibilities leads to widespread perceptions of time scarcity, and those who experience the greatest scarcity are often those most extensively enmeshed in the network of social life.[16]

The fact that there are many things to do and not enough time to do them fosters efforts to find time to do them. The reduction of time spent on the job yields more time for non-job activities. Yet competing activities must be coordinated so as to avoid chaos and to cope with the physical impossibility of being in two places at once. The schedule is the coordinating device.[17] Flexible scheduling and workers' control over the work schedule enhance the autonomous pursuit of various activities.

Individual choice may be widened or constrained depending upon the nature of the work schedule and the extent of control the individual has over it. Individuals with irregular work schedules con-trolled by their employer are limited in their pursuit of non-job activi-ties, not because they do not have time, but because timing is wrong, irregular, and unpredictable. These same workers experience a frag-mentation of time such that autonomous pursuit of non-job activities is severely circumscribed. Regular schedules, even if workers do not control them, solve some of the problems of unpredictability and frag-mentation of time.

The contrast, between those with reduced work hours who con-trol their work schedules and those on reduced hours with little or no schedule control, parallels the distinction between "old concept" and "new concept" part-time work.[18] Old concept part-time jobs are those we commonly think of when we think of part-time work. I refer to them as conventional part-time jobs. The jobs require few skills, they are poorly paid, they offer few if any fringe benefits, and they provide few avenues for advancement. Such part-time jobs are concentrated in trade and service industries and in service, sales, and clerical occupa-tions.[19] They are among the market forms of reduced work I referred to above. New concept part-time jobs are viewed as permanent, they have career potential, and the earnings package includes fringe benefits. The rate of pay in new concept part-time jobs is prorated relative to that of comparable full-time jobs, unlike old concept part-time jobs which often are in a separate track from full-time jobs and have rates of pay distinct from comparable full-time jobs. New concept part-time jobs began to appear in the late 1960s. Examples are job sharing, work sharing, and phased retirement.[20] They are the negotiated forms of reduced work I referred to above. It is in the negotiated forms, where workers may have more power vis-à-vis employers, that workers may be able to control their work schedules, thereby enhancing temporal autonomy.

French social critic André Gorz has argued that work-time reduction is an avenue toward a cultural revolution that breaks with the wage-labor system and the market economy. His admittedly utopian vision of the post-employment society does not deny the necessity to work but limits work to that which is socially necessary. By eliminating wasteful and destructive production, aggregate socially necessary work can be reduced. If socially necessary work is distributed equally across all who are able to work, the amount of work time per person would be reduced such that everyone could have more free time for autonomous pursuits. This autonomous time could be used for educational, recreational, creative, and participatory activities.

But could people afford to live on what they earn from reduced socially necessary work? Gorz says not; so individuals would be paid a social income as citizens, not a wage as workers. Thus their income would not be determined by how much they work or what they do. The employment and ecological crises in the advanced capitalist, "overdeveloped" societies are the occasion to rethink productive priorities and redivide labor. A new cultural infrastructure could be created to support autonomous activities.[21]

Gorz's vision points to the liberatory promise of reduced work. It suggests that work-time reduction can enrich both personal and social life. On this point, Gorz is in agreement with other advocates of work-time reduction. Gorz, however, observes that the cultural infrastructure currently in place, dominated by market forces, constrains the liberatory promise of reduced work. By examining individuals' experiences of reduced work as it currently exists, this book explores the empowering and disempowering qualities of reduced work.

Chapter Two

Reduced Work in Perspective

The research reported in this book is informed by three bodies of scholarship: that on labor market segmentation; work hours and work schedules; and the gender division of labor in the household. While each of these areas of inquiry bears theoretically and empirically on our understanding of gender, time, and reduced work, none is entirely adequate for that purpose. In this chapter, I discuss these bodies of literature for their contribution to an understanding of gender and reduced work, identify shortcomings of this literature as it pertains to gender and reduced work, and articulate research questions which are raised by the transformation of this literature through the lens of gender and reduced work.

Labor Market Theories

Theories of dual and segmented labor markets have incorporated part-time employment into their schemes, but have done so inadequately because of their rather narrow understanding of reduced work and because of faulty assumptions regarding the skill level of certain part-time jobs. These difficulties can be traced to the original conceptualization of these theoretical perspectives.

Labor market theories were developed by economists in reaction to human capital models of employment.[1] The human capital approach views employment outcomes as products of individual investment in education, training, or other job-related experience. Employment is the "return on investment" in certain human capital resources. Those who make better human capital investments acquire better jobs; those who do not invest adequately in human capital

15

resources acquire marginal jobs. Human capital theory has been criticized for its explanation of employment and earnings inequality between men and women. The theory suggests men hold superior jobs to women and therefore earn more because they have invested more in their human capital. The theory ignores social structural factors that would explain differences in men's and women's access to and acquisition of human capital resources, and the distribution of women and men across jobs and earnings categories.[2] It also ignores discriminatory practices that prevent or have prevented women from fully utilizing or realizing the returns from whatever human capital resources they have acquired. By extension, human capital theory would suggest that the distribution of individuals across full-time and part-time jobs, particularly the disproportionate concentration of women in part-time jobs, is also a product of human capital investment. Such an analysis ignores social structural factors, especially the gender division of labor in the household, which would explain differential access to full-time employment. Human capital theory would also explain the distribution of men and women across different categories of reduced work as a product of human capital investment. But, as I suggested in chapter one and as will become apparent in the empirical chapters that follow, reduced work, in this broad sense, is not the result of market forces alone. Workers' collective power may influence reduced work and its associated terms and conditions of employment, and this collective power intersects with the society's sex/gender system. Therefore, men may be concentrated in superior forms of reduced work, such as work sharing in manufacturing industries (with better wages and benefits), while women are concentrated in categories of reduced work (with low wages and few if any employer-provided benefits), such as conventional part-time and temporary employment.

Dual labor market theory was the first effort to improve upon the human capital approach. Doeringer and Piore argued that skills and knowledge specific to one company have grown in importance relative to transferable occupational skills.[3] Employers, therefore, are eager to retain workers who have specific knowledge and skills crucial for the smooth operation of their organization. Such workers are enticed to remain with the organization by the employer's "promise" of promotion, of a stepwise acceleration of pay, and perquisites in exchange for the worker's long-term attachment to the organization. Doeringer and Piore describe such workers as primary sector workers. They work at better paying, more secure jobs as opposed to secondary sector workers, whose jobs pay less and are insecure. Because the latter's skills are less valuable to the employer than those of primary sector workers, employers are less eager to retain secondary sector workers. The dual labor market, therefore, is divided into primary and secondary sectors and has emerged from strategies used by employers to retain the scarce labor of skilled and technical workers.[4]

While the dual labor market approach improves upon human capital theory by examining the role of employers in creating labor market outcomes for workers and recognizing the differential reward structures that employers create for differentially skilled employees, it attaches rewards to workers' skills and not to jobs per se. Thus, it is workers' skills that are differentially valued, not jobs as packages of tasks and responsibilities. As Edwards has stated in his exposition of segmented labor markets, however, "the fundamental differences are not so much among the workers as among the jobs that workers hold."[5] Therefore, the occupational structure itself is divided into segments arising "not from market forces themselves but rather from the underlying uses of labor power."[6] As Edwards has explained, the dichotomization of the economy into a monopolistic core and competitive periphery has created structural divisions in the conditions of employment. This dual economy intersects with institutionalized racism and sexism thus splintering workers into segments that constitute distinct labor markets.

Edwards identified three labor markets: the independent primary, the subordinate primary, and the secondary labor markets. Each displays qualitatively different terms of employment and reflects concentrations of workers from different racial/ethnic and gender groups such that social structural privilege or disadvantage along racial and gender lines coincides with the distribution of privilege and disadvantage in the occupational structure. The independent primary labor market consists of professional, managerial, and technical jobs for which workers must have acquired the appropriate credentials to qualify, usually post-secondary education. Located in the economy's core, these jobs pay well, include employer-provided benefits, and are reasonably secure. They provide workers with opportunities for autonomy on the job and advancement in a career progression. Examination of the statistics regarding who holds these jobs reveals that white males are disproportionately concentrated in this labor market, although women and minorities have gained limited entrance in recent decades.[7]

The subordinate primary labor market has some of the characteristics of the independent primary labor market: jobs pay reasonably well, employers provide benefits, and jobs offer some degree of long-term security. These advantages in terms of employment tend to be the product of trade unionists' efforts to win them. Also located in the economy's core, jobs in the subordinate primary labor market generally do not require the advanced formal education required in the independent primary labor market; workers can qualify for jobs in the subordinate primary labor market with high school education (or less in the past). Workers advance through seniority and skills acquired on the job. Routine production jobs in the unionized manufacturing sector and some clerical jobs exemplify the subordinate primary labor market. There are concentrations of both white and minority men in such manufacturing jobs and concentrations of white and minority women in such clerical jobs.[8] It is important to note that employment in the subordinate primary labor market has become less secure as domestic manufacturing industries have weakened competitively, as opportunities for employment have declined, and as labor unions have lost bargaining power.

The secondary labor market is comprised of "dead-end" jobs that are insecure, pay poorly, offer few if any employer-provided benefits, and offer few opportunities for advancement. Located in the economy's periphery, these jobs require little previous education or training beyond basic literacy, and they offer few opportunities to learn new skills on the job. Low-skill jobs in small, nonunion manufacturing firms; service occupations such as janitor, waitperson, orderly, and others; lower-level positions in retail and wholesale trade; low-level clerical jobs; and migrant agricultural labor are examples cited by Edwards.[9] Minorities and women tend to be concentrated in such jobs.[10]

Explicit in Edwards' analysis of segmented labor markets is declining levels of skill from the independent primary to subordinate primary to secondary labor markets. Dual and segmented labor market theories have been criticized for using skilled male labor in manufacturing as the standard by which to measure skill.[11] Mental labor of the sort common in the independent primary labor market is considered skilled labor because of the amount of formal education and imaginative effort required to perform such work and because of its relative scarcity in the labor pool. This understanding of skill in dual and segmented labor market theories does not incorporate the possibility that the emotion work involved in some service jobs, particularly that often performed by women, requires skill and acumen.[12]

Dual and segmented labor market theories can also be criticized for their treatment of reduced work. They do not differentiate among types of reduced work. They lump reduced work into a single category, that of part-time employment, and all part-time employment tends to be lumped into the secondary labor market. While it is the case that many part-time jobs, particularly in retail trade and services, are unskilled by conventional standards, low paid, insecure, and require little previous education or training, and that part-time jobs in retail trade and services constitute a large proportion of all part-time jobs, part-time professional jobs fall outside the scope of part-time employment as labor market theorists usually treat it. Part-time professionals are often paid less than their full-time counterparts, they are often excluded from employer-provided benefits, and their jobs are insecure, yet they must meet the same or nearly the same formal educational requirements as the full-time professional, and it is this formal education which Edwards takes as a defining feature of the independent primary labor market.[13] The part-time professional may also have opportunities equivalent to those of the full-time professional for creative expression and autonomy on the job. This suggests one of two things: the secondary labor market has expanded to include jobs requiring little and much formal education as a result of employers' efforts to restructure organizations in the face of recent economic difficulties, or there has emerged a secondary sector within the independent primary labor market. Empirical analysis of part-time professionals' qualifications and movement among jobs would reveal whether they move among professional and unskilled jobs as their personal circumstances dictate or whether they move among professional jobs exclusively. Such empirical analysis would yield evidence to select between those two theoretical possibilities.

Much of the foregoing discussion, as well as points made in chapter one, illustrates the conceptual difficulties that ensue when women's experiences are introduced into male-centered discourse. Traditional definitions of work focus on paid work. Traditional definitions of skill focus on craft, manual work usually performed by men. By traditional definitions, time off the job is leisure, and reduced work is unskilled. Even writers on labor market segmentation, who make a genuine effort to deal with the intersection of labor markets and the sex/gender system, fall short when it comes to the part-time professional (who is commonly a woman). It is as if part-time and professional are mutually exclusive categories.[14] This bias in the major theories of work in favor of uninterrupted full-time employment and linear careers precludes adequate treatment of reduced work and women's paid and unpaid work.

Work Hours and Work Schedules

With the exception of a cursory distinction between full-time and part-time employment, labor market theories do not customarily include work hours and work schedules among the terms and conditions of employment that are the basis for differentiating labor market sectors. Nor has such a comprehensive study of work hours and work schedules, as they relate to the various labor markets, been undertaken. The U.S. Department of Labor, however, periodically conducts surveys of work hours and work schedules and provides snapshots of the distribution of work time across the population.

Enacted in 1938, the Fair Labor Standards Act established forty hours as the legal standard for maximum weekly hours in the United States. That standard became effective in 1941, but numerous exemptions to the law limited its initial application to about one-fifth of the labor force.[15] Today the law extends to about 60 percent of all wage and salary workers.[16] The forty-hour workweek is not just a matter of law; it has become a social norm. More than half of all nonfarm wage and salary workers and roughly two-thirds of those employed full-time report that they work exactly forty hours per week. These proportions have changed little since 1973 when usual hours worked on principal jobs began being monitored through the Current Population Survey.[17]

A second standard has also emerged in the United States, that of the eight-hour day. Concerns regarding workers' health led to numerous federal and state statutes and union contracts limiting the workday to this length of time. The combination of the eight-hour day and forty-hour week have led to an implicit standard, the five-day workweek.[18] The five-day workweek is more prevalent than the forty-hour week; in 1985 almost three-fourths of the work force, and more than four-fifths of those employed full-time, reported schedules of five working days. Both mean (4.9) and median (5.5) usual days per week have remained nearly constant since 1973.[19]

Most Americans work Monday through Friday; however, Saturday work is the usual routine for one-fourth of all workers, and one in eight report they usually work on Sunday.[20] Weekend work is especially common in the retail trade industry. Retail sales workers, who represent about 17 percent of the weekday work force, account for more than one-third of the population active in their main job on weekends.[21] Of the wage and salary workers who must be on the job on weekends, a disproportionate share are employed part-time. On Saturday, the percentage of overall employment accounted for by prime-aged men holds steady with that during the week. That of prime-aged women drops sharply, but the proportionate decline is offset by greater representation of teens, young adults, and men aged sixty-five and over. On Sundays, the proportion of prime-aged male workers declines and that of prime-aged women increases along with teens, young adults, and older men.[22]

Of those respondents to a recent Current Population Survey who reported variable day schedules, 28 percent cited voluntary reasons. Of the 72 percent citing involuntary reasons, nine of ten cited the schedule as a requirement of the job; most of the remainder reported they worked shifts because they could not find any other job.[23]

Work outside the typical daylight hours—usually in the evening—is the usual routine for about one-sixth of full-time workers and one-half of part-time workers.[24] Nearly one-fifth of part-time workers have some type of flexible scheduling.[25] By contrast, about 12 percent of all full-time wage and salary workers have flexible schedules.[26]

Flexible schedules are fairly common in the federal government.[27] In the private sector, they occur more frequently in service-producing industries rather than goods-producing industries.[28] Surprisingly, given the common assumptions that mothers need and can get flexible employment, men are more likely than women to have flexibility in their work schedules. This is true for both full and part-time workers.[29]

Because work-time occupies a large portion of our waking hours and work schedules often dictate the rhythm of life, work schedules have considerable influence on the rest of life. They shape the availability of time for off-the-job activities. As Linder has suggested, work-time "affects both the supply and demand for time on other activities."[30] Taking employment as one of numerous activities that occupy Americans' time, Robinson developed a schematic model of factors affecting time use, including resource factors (income, appliances, automobiles, etc.), personal factors (sex, age, education), role factors (employment, marriage, parenthood), and environmental factors (day of week, geographic location, weather, emergencies, etc.).[31] In his empirical test of that model, Robinson found that role factors influenced time use more than any other set of factors, with employment having the greatest effect followed by parenthood and then marital roles. As might be expected, parental and marital roles demanded proportionately more from women than from men. Among the personal factors influencing time use, sex and education had the strongest effects.[32] The sex differences reported by Robinson are important and will be explored further in the section on household work that follows.

Robinson's data were collected in the mid-1960s, and they reflect the gender relations of that era. More recent research on the gender division of labor in households will help us assess how much those gender relations have shifted.

While employment was the most important role factor influencing time use in his study, Robinson did not explore work schedules per se nor did he systematically compare full-time and part-time workers, although he did briefly compare workers on four-day and five-day, full-time workweeks (finding little difference between them in their use of time). With broad brush strokes, he distinguished employed men from employed women and housewives and noted some tendency for employed women to work shorter hours than employed men.[33] Since Robinson's path-clearing study, a spate of research has been carried out exploring the effects of work schedules on family life. Women's increased participation in the paid labor force and the increase in the number of dual-earner households have fueled interest in this area of research.

In the 1950s and 1960s, research on work schedules was concerned primarily with shiftwork and flexitime. Generally, studies have shown that shiftwork interferes with family life, unless workers can select their shifts, and male shiftworkers' wives perform considerable adaptive work to create a "normal" family life. Flexitime increases family time by small amounts and is related to lower work/family conflict except among workers for whom flexitime does not relieve the stress of major family responsibilities.[34]

The first comprehensive effort to measure systematically the relationship between work schedules and family life was undertaken by Staines and Pleck.[35] Using data from the 1977 Quality of Employment Survey, they explored four aspects of work schedules for their effects on family life: pattern of days worked each week, pattern of hours worked each day, number of hours worked each week, and flexibility of work schedules. Family life was assessed in terms of amount of time spent in child care and housework, interference between work and family life, and levels of family adjustment.[36] Among their major findings were that nonstandard patterns of days each week (weekend work, variable patterns of days), nonstandard patterns of hours each day (shiftwork), and working a large number of hours each week have a negative influence on workers' family lives, especially among workers who have the least control over their schedules. Among workers who reported a high degree of control over their work schedules, weekend work, shiftwork, and long hours were not as detrimental to family life.

Another important contribution of the Staines and Pleck study is its systematic examination of work schedules and family life among dual-earner couples. In more than half of the dual-earner couples in their sample, the husband was employed more hours each week than the wife. Husband and wife worked a simlar number of hours in 32 percent of the couples, and the wife worked more hours in 11.6 percent.[37] They also found that the effects of one spouse's job schedule went beyond that individual's own family life and extended to the other spouse's job schedule and family life. Specifically, they reported that one spouse's schedule may influence the other spouse's work schedule, and one spouse's stressful schedule may reduce the quality of family life experienced by the other spouse.[38]

While workers with part-time schedules of twenty hours or more each week were included in their sample, Staines and Pleck did not systematically compare part-time workers to full-time workers, nor did they distinguish among different types of less-than-full-time employment. Such analyses would tell us whether and to what extent family life is improved by shorter hours and would assess the different effects of varied forms of reduced work. As my research suggests, some types of reduced work permit workers to control their schedules more than others, some types of reduced work are more secure than others, and some types of reduced work are more attractive financially than others. Given these variations among different forms of reduced work, what features of reduced work might negate any improvement in family life that results from reduced hours? Because reduced work intersects with the sex/gender system such that women tend to be concentrated in certain types of reduced work while men are concentrated in others, might the rewards and costs of reduced work be distributed unequally to men and women? If reduced work improves family life, does it improve the family lives of men and women equally? Such questions need more empirical study.

The Gender Division of Labor in the Household

The preceding discussion of work hours and work schedules, of course, considered only paid employment. Because those who work less than full-time report using much of their time off the job in household work activities, it is important to examine what is known from scholarly studies about women's and men's contributions to household work.

Berk provides an excellent review of the scholarship on household work in her book, *The Gender Factory*.[39] While there are methodological and conceptual differences among the numerous studies that have been conducted on the subject, some generalities can be drawn regarding who does what and how much in married-couple households. Estimates of wives' work time in the household range from thirty to sixty hours per week depending upon whether they are employed, how many children they have and their ages, and how researchers measured household work. On average, wives' contribution to household work constitutes about 70 percent of the total time that all members spend engaged in household work. While the content of household work has changed historically, the total time spent on it remains unchanged as does women's disproportionate responsibility for carrying out household tasks.[40]

Variations in wives' household work time generally are not explained by variations in the contributions of other household members. This is readily apparent upon examination of the scholarship on husbands' contributions to household work. As Berk states, "In a great number of studies, using quite disparate methods, the level of husbands' contributions consistently appears to be small," and differences in husbands' paid work time produce very little variation in the amount of time they dovote to household work.[41] Husbands devote between ten and fifteen hours per week to household work, constituting about 15 percent of the total time devoted by all household members. Notably, husbands' contributions vary little whether their wives are employed or not. In a rather startling finding, Walker and Woods reported that wives with the longest workweeks, wage work and household work combined, were those married to men with the shortest workweeks as measured by wage work and household work.[42] Hartmann, arguing that men benefit directly from women's labor, has suggested that husbands require more household work than they contribute. Noting that single women spend considerably less time on housework than wives with families of the same size and wives who are employed, she speculates that the difference in time spent on housework (approximately eight hours per week) could be interpreted as the amount of increased housework caused by the husband's presence.[43] If what Hartmann suggests is true, the husbands with short workweeks in the Walker and Woods study may have spent more time at home without increasing their contribution to household work and perhaps created more, rather than less, household work for their wives. Walker and Woods also found that husbands' total work time tended to decrease as wives' hours of employment increased, suggesting that husbands reduce their involvement in paid employment as wives increase theirs.[44]

Research further suggests that wives who are employed outside the home have the longest workweeks, wage work and household work combined (sixty-five to seventy hours per week when they are employed fifteen hours or more per week), although they spend comparatively less time on household work than their unemployed counterparts. Instead of other household members taking up the slack in household work when wives are employed, wives cut corners in completing household tasks. Still, there is evidence that wives sacrifice much weekend leisure time to household work.[45] As my interviews reported in this book reveal, wives who choose to be employed less than full-time recoup some of that weekend leisure time by doing more household work during the week. Such work time reduction is an adjustment *women* make to relieve their double burden, and it appears that men make few modifications in their time use to relieve their wives of excess domestic responsibility.

Pleck's research, however, suggests that the recent changes in women's status in society, particularly their greater participation in the paid labor force, are contributing to a shift in men's roles, particularly greater involvement in families. He reports that the amount of time husbands devote to family work, narrowly defined, has increased in recent years, such that the difference between employed wives' total work (wage and household combined) and their husband's is only twelve minutes a day.[46] Using a broader definition of family work, however, Pleck reports a difference between employed wives and husbands of about 2.2 hours per day. Disparities between husbands' and wives' housework are quite small, but with regard to child care the disparities are much greater with the lion's share of the responsibility for child care falling on the wives' shoulders. Pleck concludes that "[E]mployed wives' overload has been mitigated in direct housework and childcare activities, but not in the broader range of these activities that actually constitute the vast majority of all family work."[47] Other research suggests that fathers of very young children are spending significantly more time in family roles than they used to, while there has been little or no change in fathers of older children.[48] Although Pleck is optimistic that men and women are moving toward convergence in their family time, discrepancies in the proportion of time they devote to paid work and family work persist.[49] As my research suggests and as Pleck explains, employed wives' overload diminishes because they make adjustments in their paid work time. Wives' time devoted to paid work as well as continuity of employment over time are, generally, substantially less than husbands', but this results in disadvantages for wives in terms of marginal employment status, lower wages, economic vulnerability in the husband's absence, and inadequate or nonexistent pension rights.[50] Such marginal economic status combined with disproportionate responsibility for household work may contribute to greater morbidity among women.[51]

The discrepancies between husbands' and wives' participation in and responsibility for child care suggest that sex-typing persists in the allocation of tasks in the household. Meissner notes a male preference for functionally specific tasks with clear and identifiable boundaries, greater discretion in how and when to complete tasks, and greater leisure components.[52] This characterization of men's household work is wholly consistent with my male informants' descriptions of their "household projects." Men tend to perform household tasks that require undivided attention for a specified period of time and that, when completed, need not be done again for as much as a week, a month, a year, or even longer (such as mowing the lawn, vehicle maintenance, household repairs and improvements, and the like).

There is some evidence, however, of task convergence among women and men. Surveys conducted by the University of Michigan and the University of Maryland suggest that men are doing a larger proportion of meal preparation, bill paying, and cleaning than twenty-five years ago, although women still complete the majority of these tasks. Women, however, are doing somewhat fewer of the outdoor chores and household repairs than twenty-five years ago, while men report doing somewhat more.[53]

Most scholars have explained the consistent inequities between women and men in the household division of labor by more abstract cultural notions of men's and women's roles in society. The traditional breadwinner role has led men to direct their family responsibilities to an arena outside the household, while the traditional homemaker role has led women to focus their energies inside the home. Pleck's statistical analysis of who does what and how much in the household confirms the importance of social constructions of gender, relative to time devoted to paid work. Although there are important methodological differences in the two data sets he examines, Pleck finds that, overall, sex accounts for more variance in family work than does paid work, and variations in paid work have more impact on wives' family work than husbands'.[54] The latter finding is consistent with that of Walker and Woods mentioned above, that as wives' hours of employment increase the amount of time they devote to household work decreases. Pleck also reports that men's and women's sex role attitudes have little influence on the household division of labor.[55] Therefore, the household division of labor in homes where husbands and wives espouse gender egalitarian ideologies differs little from that in homes where husbands and wives espouse traditional gender ideologies.

Studies that explore the effects of paid work time on household work, such as those by Walker and Woods and Pleck, have not explicitly compared part-time and full-time workers.[56] Because the vast majority of studies tend to distinguish dual-earner from sole-breadwinner households, variations among dual-earner households are not examined in great detail. This shortcoming makes it difficult to understand if and how much the gender division of labor in the household differs in homes where at least one earner is employed part-time, where the part-time worker is male, where the part-time worker is female, where both earners are employed part-time, and where both earners are employed full-time. My research, discussed in this book, does not systematically compare such households either, but the individual accounts of my informants suggest that wives who are employed less than full-time are disproportionately responsible for household work, wives use less-than-full-time employment to accommodate their household responsibilities, and husbands' less-than-full-time employment does not significantly alter the nature of their contributions to running and maintaining a household even when they devote more time to household work. Thus it appears that the allocation of tasks in most dual-earner households remains quite sex-segregated under conditions of less-than-full-time employment whether men or women are employed less than full-time.

Further, there is limited scholarship on the influence of specific types of work schedules on household work. Among the dual-earner couples in the data sets they analyzed, Staines and Pleck found that regular weekend work is associated with decreased time in child care and housework, especially among husbands. A variable pattern of days worked each week predicts less time in child care and, in an odd crossover effect, wives' variable day patterns reduce husbands' time in housework. For the total sample, of which dual-earner couples were a subset, non-daytime and variable shifts were associated with more time in housework.[57] The latter is consistent with my finding that people working less than full-time with variable schedules devote much time off the job to household work. This appears to occur because time fragmentation resulting from variable schedules limits people to off-the-job activities that can be undertaken spontaneously. Housework is such an activity. It is everpresent and malleable, thus it can be undertaken spontaneously and adapted to fill the available time.

This chapter has provided a scholarly context for locating my study of gender and reduced work. As I have suggested, reduced work exists within a larger set of social relations characterized by gender inequality and labor market segmentation. These relations influence the nature of reduced work, associated work schedules, income, and individuals' quality of life. The empirical chapters that follow examine these phenomena in order to more fully understand men's and women's experiences of reduced work.

Chapter Three

How the Study was Done

In this study I was concerned with individuals' experiences of reduced work. I explored a number of questions pertaining to their employment and use of time off the job. What sorts of jobs did they have? How much did they earn? What were their work schedules like? How much control did they have over their work schedules? How did they use their time off the job? Did working less than full-time seem to enrich or impoverish their quality of life? What difference did it make if the worker was female or male?

Because my research emphasized people's experiences, I conducted qualitative, in-depth interviews with a total of forty-four women and men who were employed less than full-time when I met them. I wanted to hear their stories as they would tell them; I did not want to collapse their experiences into predetermined categories as would have been the case if I had asked close-ended questions. To prompt them to tell me their stories, I asked a series of open-ended questions to sensitize them to my curiosities. I asked the same questions to each person I interviewed, ensuring comparability across interviews, although questions were not necessarily asked in the same sequence. I wanted the interviews to have a conversational tone, so I posed questions when they seemed pertinent to the topics that had arisen. I also wanted the flexibility to stray from a predetermined set of questions that I might follow leads provided by my informants. To impose a rigid sequence of questions would have interrupted the natural flow of conversation and restricted the information to which I would have access.

Each interview developed a common rhythm. I began each interview by asking my informant about his or her current job. That usually led us to discuss my informant's particular responsibilities, how and why the job was acquired, the work schedule, previous work history, and the like. After we had thoroughly discussed my informant's employment, we shifted gears to explore his or her use of time off the job. That topic shift usually occurred at a point about midway through the interview. During this portion of the interview, we discussed child care responsibilities, household work, relationships with other household members, relationships with kin outside the household, relationships with friends, recreation, education, community service, and so on. At the conclusion of the interview I asked each informant two summary questions. First I asked, "Is there anything else about your job or your work schedule that you want to share with me?" Then I asked, "Is there anything else about your use of time off the job that we have not discussed that you would like to discuss?" These summary questions were designed to tap issues important to my informants that I had not been able to anticipate prior to or during the course of the interview. They were my effort to ensure that I had left no stone unturned.

Near the end of each interview I asked my informants to complete a short, close-ended questionnaire to gather basic demographic and household data. I held this item until near the end of the interview because it asked potentially sensitive questions about, for example, income and marital status. I wanted to ensure the establishment of sufficient trust between interviewer and informant before discussing such matters. Often, however, the information asked for on the questionnaire had been uncovered earlier in the interview. Completing the questionnaire became an opportunity to verify information and sometimes triggered additional comment on a topic.

The interviews, conducted with volunteers and averaging ninety minutes in length, were completed between September 1986 and October 1987. Most took place in a small meeting room on the large midwestern university campus where I worked. In some cases they took place in a private meeting room at the informant's place of employment. A few interviews took place at the informant's home, and a couple were conducted over the phone. The work sharers were interviewed in an office generously provided for that purpose by the union local.

The research method I used is best interpreted as a cooperative venture, or meeting of the minds, between informant and interviewer. I deliberately use the term informants instead of subject to emphasize their knowledge of their experiences of reduced work and to avoid defining their role as a passive one. I brought my sociological imagination to the endeavor, a perspective that my informants lacked, but their intimate knowledge of reduced work is what I lacked.[1] My socio-logical imagination complements the experiences of my informants, yielding new insight into the sociological meaning of people's varied experiences of reduced work.

This study was also conducted in the spirit of critical social science. Accordingly, it seeks to interpret a social phenomenon to promote social change. As Fay explains, critical social science values collective autonomy. It promotes self-determination and the removal of barriers that prevent people from living in accordance with their will. Critical social science promotes the transformation of social institutions and social relations such that they permit greater self-determination.[2]

Specific to this project, work schedules are conceived of as dominating forces that may inhibit people's use of time off the job and, therefore, personal autonomy. In what ways does reduced work influence the work schedule, both its nature and the ability of individual workers to determine their own work schedule? Does controlling the work schedule, by definition, enhance personal autonomy? Does this differ for women and men? If workers are poorly paid or their incomes are irregular, does financial insecurity override any autonomy gained by controlling the work schedule? To what extent might controlling the work schedule empower individuals in the management of their daily lives? These are the sorts of questions this study addresses in order to understand, at a theoretical level, the relationship between gender, time, and reduced work.

Sample Construction and Characteristics

Following the tenets of grounded theory, the sample was constructed using a theoretical sampling procedure.[3] Theoretical sampling is a process followed by researchers who want to generate theory rather than verify it. Researchers sample theoretically not to achieve the broadest coverage of a population for representational purposes, but to identify the properties of theoretical categories and the interrelationships among them. It requires only collecting data on categories for the generation of properties, not the fullest statistical coverage of a group.[4]

In this project I sampled four different types of reduced work to develop a theoretical understanding of each type and, through comparative analysis, a theoretical understanding of reduced work more broadly. I compared the types of jobs and levels of pay within each. I was also curious about the nature of work schedules within each and workers' ability to control their work schedules. I compared these characteristics across types of reduced work to develop a richer understanding of reduced work in contemporary American society. I also compared the distribution of women and men across each type of reduced work to understand how reduced work affects the use of time off the job and, by extension, personal autonomy among women and men. I looked for people within each type of reduced work with regular schedules and irregular ones, who controlled their work schedule and who did not, to see just how reduced work affects workers' quality of life.

Because my sample is theoretically constructed, it is not a scientific sample in that it is not representative of all part-time workers, temporary employees, job sharers, and work sharers. Therefore, findings from this study are not necessarily intended to be generalized to the population of workers in these four categories of reduced work. This study does not assert and test hypotheses about the relationship between reduced work, personal autonomy, and use of time off the job, although my findings may generate them. Instead, my goal was to understand people's experience of reduced work to determine conditions that enhance or impede personal autonomy and the use of time off the job. I tapped different types of reduced work in my sample in an effort to determine how variations in the type of reduced work might affect work schedules, income, personal autonomy, and use of time off the job.

While the sample may not be representative of all part-time workers, temporaries, job sharers, and work sharers, I am confident that my informants were typical of workers in those categories. For example, women predominated among the part-time workers, temporaries, and job sharers and men predominated among the work sharers. This is consistent with the distribution of women and men across categories of reduced work as I will report in chapters four through seven. The occupations held by my informants are also typical of those employed in these types of reduced work.

In the sections that follow, I develop a demographic profile of each of the four groups of workers who shared with me their experiences of reduced work. These profiles illuminate the similarities and differences among the groups that composed the sample for this study.

The Part-Time Workers

I recruited part-time workers to interview from several public and private-sector establishments. Because large numbers of part-time workers are employed in health care industries and retailing, I concentrated my recruitment energies at establishments of that type: At a private hospital I recruited nurses and clerical workers; at a chain department store I recruited sales workers; at a discount department store I also recruited sales workers. Through a friend, I met a man who worked seasonally for the city. His work schedule differed from that of the other part-time workers and provided a theoretically interesting point of contrast. All told, I spoke with nine part-time workers; seven women and two men. All of the part-time workers in my sample were white.

The part-time workers' median age was twenty-seven years, ranging from twenty to forty-six. This is the second youngest group in my sample. The part-time workers were somewhat older than the temporaries but younger than the job sharers and work sharers.

As Table 1 illustrates, about half of the part-time workers were high school graduates. The remainder had completed some college or had graduated from college and completed some graduate training.

Most of the part-time workers were clerical and sales workers. Two were in skilled trades (gardening/landscaping and tailoring), and one was a professional (nurse). Two members of the sample claimed their part-time job as a second job. One of these two was also employed full-time as a clerical worker; the other was also employed full-time as a school teacher.

Earnings from part-time jobs ranged from less than five thousand dollars to just under twenty thousand dollars annually among the members of my sample. About half of the part-time workers I interviewed earned between ten thousand and fifteen thousand dollars a year from their part-time job. These earnings place the part-time workers in my sample behind the job sharers and work sharers. This is explained by differences in type of occupation and by labor union membership. Approximately half of the part-time workers were covered by a collective bargaining agreement. (The same proportion of the job sharers and all of the work sharers were union members.)

About half of the part-time workers were married at the time I interviewed them. The remainder were either divorced, never married, or cohabiting. All of the part-time workers who were married were women living in dual-earner households. One woman was the sole head of household. The other part-time workers were sharing households with parents or other unrelated adults.

The Temporaries

I recruited temporaries to interview from two temporary help supply (THS) companies. Names were selected randomly from the compa-

Table 1 Characteristics of the Sample of Part-Time Workers
(N = 9)

AGE	M	F	EDUCATION	M	F
18–25	1	2	Less than HS	0	0
26–30	0	3	HS graduate	0	4
31–40	1	1	Some college	2	1
41–50	0	1	BA/BS	0	0
51–60	0	0	Some graduate school	0	2
			MA/MS	0	0

OCCUPATION	M	F	INCOME	M	F
Professional	0	1	Less than $5,000	0	1
Clerical	0	3	$5,000–$9,999	0	2
Sales	1	2	$10,000–$14,999	2	2
Skilled	1	1	$15,000–$19,999	0	2

UNION MEMBERSHIP	M	F	MARITAL STATUS	M	F
Yes	2	2	Married	0	4
No	0	5	Never Married	1	1
			Divorced	0	1
			Cohabiting	1	1

HOUSEHOLD TYPE	M	F
Husband-wife Households		
Husband sole earner	0	—
Dual-earner	0	4
Wife sole earner	—	0
Female-headed,		
no husband present	—	1
Single	0	0
Shares household with		
parents or other		
unrelated adult(s)	2	2

nies' active files, and letters were sent to them briefly describing the research project and requesting voluntary participation. Twelve temporaries were interviewed; nine women and three men. One of the twelve was a black woman. One of the men was Hispanic.

The temporaries were the youngest of the four groups of workers I interviewed. Their median age was twenty-four years. The age range among the temporaries was the widest of the four groups, from eighteen to fifty-nine years.

As Table 2 illustrates, one-third of the temporaries were high school graduates, and one-half had completed some college. One temporary had a bachelor's degree, and one had a master's. Two-thirds of the temporaries worked as clerical workers. One man worked as a laborer. Three temporaries (one-fourth of the sample) had no placement at the time I interviewed them. Of those three, one man and one woman preferred clerical work and one man preferred labor or service jobs.

It was difficult to determine annual income among the temporaries I interviewed because their employment was often intermittent and unpredictable. Overall, they reported earning from $3.25 to $5.00 an hour depending on the nature of their placement. Two women who had worked forty-hour weeks for several months at clerical jobs estimated that their annual earnings would be around twelve thousand dollars if they continued to work forty-hour weeks regularly. Data published by the U.S. Bureau of Labor Statistics indicate that employees in the THS industry earned an average weekly income of $187 and an average annual income of $9,713 in 1986, the year I conducted most of my interviews. In Michigan, where my informants lived, temporaries' wages were slightly higher than the national average that year, $191 a week or $9,925 annually.[5] None of the temporaries I interviewed was represented by a labor union.

Five of the temporaries I interviewed had never been married; four were married; two were divorced; and one was cohabiting. The four who were married lived in husband-wife households; of them, three lived in dual-earner households. In one husband-wife household, the wife was the sole earner. Two of the temporaries I interviewed were single and lived alone. Six shared a household with parents or other unrelated adults.

The Job Sharers

I recruited job sharers through the State of Michigan Department of Civil Service. Job sharing tends to be an individually negotiated employment arrangement, and a minority of private companies permit

Table 2   Characteristics of the Sample of Temporaries
(N = 12)

AGE	M	F	EDUCATION	M	F
18–25	0	7	Less than HS	0	0
26–30	0	0	HS graduate	2	2
31–40	1	2	Some college	1	5
41–50	1	0	BA/BS	0	1
51–60	1	0	Some graduate school	0	0
			MA/MS	0	1

OCCUPATION	M	F	MARITAL STATUS	M	F
Clerical	0	8	Married	1	3
Laborers	1	0	Divorced	1	1
No placement	2	1	Never Married	0	5
			Cohabiting	1	0

HOUSEHOLD TYPE	M	F
Husband-wife Households		
Husband sole earner	0	—
Dual-earner	1	2
Wife sole earner	—	1
Female-headed,		
no husband present	—	0
Single	1	1
Shares household with		
parents or other		
unrelated adult(s)	1	5

it.[6] Therefore, it can be difficult to identify job sharers and organizations that permit job sharing. Because I knew the State of Michigan permitted job sharing, and because I anticipated that there would be a relatively large number of job sharers in state government, I chose to concentrate my recruitment energies there. One job sharer in the sample was not a state government employee, however. She was employed at a private hospital and was recruited initially as a part-time worker.

During the course of her interview, I discovered that she actually shared her job. I include her in the sample of job sharers because her experience illustrates the similarities of job sharing across organizational settings. All told, I interviewed eleven job sharers (nine women and two men), ten of whom were white and one of whom was black.

The job sharers' median age was thirty-three years. They ranged in age from twenty-seven to fifty-three years. All of the job sharers were high school graduates, and many had attended college although they had not completed four-year degrees. Three job sharers had completed college or pursued some graduate training. As a group, the job sharers had the most formal education of all of the groups I interviewed. Their relatively high level of education correlates somewhat with the types of occupations they held. Four of the eleven were in occupations that would be categorized as professional. The remaining seven (all women) were in clerical occupations.

As Table 3 further illustrates, the job sharers were also among the better paid workers in my sample, although they were not as well paid as the work sharers. Annual income among the job sharers ranged from ten thousand to twenty-five thousand dollars. Five of the eleven were represented by a labor union. The state government employees who were not represented were excluded from the bargaining unit because of the types of jobs they held. Individuals who were accountants, for example, performed work deemed to be confidential and, therefore, they were excluded from contract coverage.

Ten of the eleven job sharers were married at the time I interviewed them and one was cohabiting. All eleven lived in dual-earner households.

The Work Sharers

In this study the work sharers were a group of autoworkers who volunteered to be laid off temporarily under an inverse seniority layoff scheme established at the plant where they were employed. Ordinarily autoworkers are laid off in order of seniority from low to high. Under the inverse scheme, high seniority workers volunteered for temporary layoff for periods of four months, seven months, or one year depending upon their level of seniority and job classification. I recruited work sharers to interview with the cooperation of the United Auto Workers (UAW) local that had negotiated the inverse-seniority layoff plan with General Motors. We sent letters to randomly selected participants in the inverse layoff scheme explaining the research project and requesting volunteers. In the end, I interviewed twelve work

Table 3 Characteristics of the Sample of Job Sharers
(N = 11)

AGE	M	F	EDUCATION	M	F
18–25	0	0	Less than HS	0	0
26–30	0	4	HS graduate	0	1
31–40	1	4	Some college	0	7
41–50	0	1	BA/BS	1	1
51–60	1	0	Some graduate school	1	0
			MA/MS	0	0

OCCUPATION	M	F	INCOME	M	F
Professional	2	2	$10,000–$14,999	1	6
Clerical	0	7	$15,000–$19,999	1	2
			$20,000–$24,999	0	1

UNION MEMBERSHIP	M	F	MARITAL STATUS	M	F
Yes	1	4	Married	1	9
No	1	5	Divorced	0	0
			Never Married	0	0
			Cohabiting	1	0

HOUSEHOLD TYPE	M	F
Husband-wife Households		
Husband sole earner	0	—
Dual-earner	1	9
Wife sole earner	—	0
Female-headed,		
no husband present	—	0
Single	0	0
Shares household with		
parents or other		
unrelated adult(s)	1	0

Table 4 Characteristics of the Sample of Work Sharers
(N = 12)

AGE	M	F	EDUCATION	M	F
18–25	0	0	Less than HS	5	0
26–30	0	0	HS graduate	3	2
31–40	3	2	Some college	2	0
41–50	3	0	BA/BS	0	0
51–60	4	0	Some graduate school	0	0
			MA/MS	0	0

OCCUPATION	M	F	INCOME	M	F
Operatives	5	0	$25,000–$29,999	2	1
Laborers	5	2	$30,000–$34,999	5	1
			$35,000–$39,999	1	0
			$40,000–$44,999	1	0
			$45,000–$49,999	1	0

UNION MEMBERSHIP	M	F	MARITAL STATUS	M	F
Yes	10	2	Married	6	2
No	0	0	Divorced	4	0
			Never Married	0	0
			Cohabiting	0	0

HOUSEHOLD TYPE	M	F
Husband-wife Households		
Husband sole earner	4	—
Dual-earner	2	2
Wife sole earner	—	0
Female-headed,		
no husband present	—	0
Single	2	0
Shares household with		
parents or other		
unrelated adult(s)	2	0

sharers (two women and ten men). Ten of the twelve were white; one was black and another, Hispanic.

The work sharers were the oldest group of workers I interviewed, with a median age of forty-two years. They ranged in age from thirty-three to fifty-five years. They had the least formal education of all of the groups of workers I interviewed. Five work sharers (all men) had not graduated from high school, five had completed high school, and two had attended college for a brief period of time. All of the work sharers were production workers in the automobile plant. Seven of the twelve were laborers, and five were operatives. One of the operatives was also a self-employed tax consultant. They had been autoworkers for fourteen to thirty years and represented career stages from the midpoint to near retirement.

The work sharers were the highest paid group in my sample. The bottom end of their income range started where the job sharers topped out, at twenty-five thousand dollars annually. The work sharers earned as high as fifty thousand dollars annually. Half earned from thirty thousand to thirty-five thousand dollars a year. All of the work sharers were union members.

Two-thirds of the work sharers were married when I interviewed them, and one-third were divorced. Of the eight living in husband-wife households, four men were sole earners, and two men and two women lived in dual-earner households. Of the four who were divorced, two lived alone and two shared a household with parents or other unrelated adults.

These profiles reveal important differences in age, education, type of occupation, income, union membership, marital status, and household structure across types of reduced work. Gender differences across types of reduced work are also noteworthy, with women concentrated among the conventional part-time workers, the temporaries, and the job sharers. Men were concentrated among the work sharers I studied.

How did these groups of individuals experience reduced work? Did they find it an enriching source of autonomy and balance in their lives, or were their lives impoverished literally and figuratively by reduced work? The empirical analysis of these questions begins in the next chapter.

Chapter Four

The Part-Time Workers

Some twenty million people were employed part-time in the United States in 1988, representing about 20 percent of the civilian labor force. About three-fourths of those workers were employed part-time by choice. The remaining one-fourth were employed part-time because their hours had been reduced due to slack work or because they were unable to find full-time employment.[1]

Part-time employment is defined by the U.S. Bureau of Labor Statistics as employment for less than thirty-five hours per week. Part-time jobs have grown more rapidly than full-time jobs since the mid-1950s. Between the mid-1950s and the late 1970s, the number of part-time employees in nonagricultural industries increased at an average annual rate of nearly four percent, more than double the rate of increase for full-time workers.[2] More recently, much of the increase in part-time employment can be attributed to growth in involuntary part-time employment.[3] Since 1970, the proportion of the total labor force employed part-time voluntarily has remained between 13 and 14 percent. The proportion employed part-time involuntarily, however, has almost doubled, increasing from 3.1 percent in 1970 to 5.7 percent in 1984.[4]

Nine to Five, the National Association of Working Women, estimates that more than 25 percent of the nearly ten million jobs created during the first half of the 1980s were part-time.[5] Wider Opportunities for Women reports that the involuntary part-time segment of the work force grew 60 percent between 1979 and 1985, with three-fourths of the part-time jobs created since 1981 filled by involuntary part-time employees.[6] Historically, the number of people employed part-time for economic reasons has fluctuated in direct relation to the number of unemployed persons in the United States, suggesting involuntary part-time employment, like the unemployment rate, is an indicator of the relative health of the nation's economy.[7] The significant increase in recent years in the proportion of the labor force involuntarily employed part-time supports the notion that the national economy is in a protracted period of structural transformation and crisis.

Most part-time workers are women, teenagers, and older persons. Of this group, women are the largest proportion, constituting two-thirds of all part-time workers. This proportion has held steady since 1968, the first year for which such data are available. As Table 5 further illustrates, women are also about two-thirds of voluntary part-time workers. Men claim a larger proportion of involuntary than voluntary part-time employment, constituting almost half of all involuntary part-time workers. Women are slightly more than half of all involuntary part-time workers.

As noted above, we have seen dramatic increases in involuntary part-time work in recent decades. Figures reported in Table 6 show that involuntary part-time employment grew 190 percent from 1968 to 1988. Among men, involuntary part-time employment grew 175 percent during the same period, and it grew 202 percent among women. These rates of growth in involuntary part-time employment far exceed the rates of growth in part-time employment overall and voluntary part-time employment during the same twenty-year period.

Part-time employment tends to be concentrated within certain industries and among particular types of jobs. Part-time jobs comprise 30 percent of the jobs in the services industry and more than 50 percent of the jobs in retail trade. Nearly half of all part-time workers are in sales and service occupations.[8]

It is commonly believed that part-time employment has grown in response to increased demand from workers who want part-time jobs. While it is true that some individuals work part-time voluntarily, the fact that they seek part-time jobs does not necessarily explain why employers want to hire part-time workers. And as noted above, the recent growth in involuntary part-time employment suggests that the supply of part-time jobs exceeds the demand for such jobs. Quite simply, the supply of part-time jobs has increased because companies want to reduce their labor costs. The drive to reduce labor costs is especially pronounced in labor-intensive industries such as retail trade and services, sectors of the U.S. economy that have grown rapidly in the post-World War II era. Employers can reduce labor costs by employing a larger proportion of part-time workers because part-time workers' base pay is usually less than that of full-time workers and they often do not receive company-provided employee benefits. Part-

Table 5   Men and Women as a Percentage of Part-Time Workers, 1968–1988.

	% OF ALL		% OF VOL		% OF INVOL[1]	
	1968	1988	1968	1988	1968	1988
Men	35	33	34	31	48	46
Women	65	67	66	69	52	54

1. Part-time for economic reasons, usually work full time and usually work part time.

Calculations based on data reported in U.S. Department of Labor, Bureau of Labor Statistics, *Handbook of Labor Statistics* (Washington, DC: GPO, 1989), Tables 12 and 23.

Table 6   Rates of Change in Part-Time Employment among Men and Women, 1968–1988

Total Part-Time	86%
Men	73%
Women	92%
Voluntary Part-Time	68%
Men	51%
Women	76%
Involuntary Part-Time[1]	190%
Men	175%
Women	202%

1. Part-time for economic reasons, usually work full time and usually work part time.

Calculations based on data reported in U.S. Department of Labor, Bureau of Labor Statistics, *Handbook of Labor Statistics* (Washington, DC: GPO, 1989), Tables 12 and 23.

time workers earn about 60 percent of the hourly wages of full-time workers.[9] Seventy-five percent of part-time, year-round workers receive no health insurance, while 88 percent who work less than a full year get no health insurance.[10] Less than 20 percent of part-time workers are included in pension programs.[11] Nonprofessional part-time jobs, in particular, tend to be low-paying jobs with few fringe benefits.[12] Part-time workers who are covered by a collective bargaining agreement are exceptions in that they tend to receive higher base pay and some benefits by comparison to nonunion part-time workers.[13] The differential wage rates paid to part-time workers compared to full-time workers may also depress full-time wage rates, contributing to a further reduction of an employer's total wage bill. The latter explains why some labor unions oppose part-time employment.

Employers hire part-time workers to create a flexible work force in addition to reducing labor costs. Unlike most full-time workers, part-time workers can be scheduled to cover peak demand periods during the day, their weekly hours can be expanded during periods of increased demand, and their hours can be contracted during slack periods.[14] This flexibility permits employers to be responsive to market conditions without maintaining a bulky full-time work force. The use of part-time workers allows managers to trim their permanent, full-time work force, thereby decreasing the number of workers to whom they are obligated and reducing the total wage bill. Politically, it may mean fewer workers to layoff in periods of economic recession because part-time workers' hours can be reduced further, although collective bargaining contracts covering part-time employment may establish floors for minimum weekly hours.

The existence of a part-time work force also enhances management control of labor. Full-time workers who fear a reduction in their hours may be more compliant workers, and part-time workers who want more hours may kowtow to the dictates of management in the hope of acquiring more work hours or even a full-time job. Despite the latters' hopes, however, the restructuring of work associated with the employment of more contingent workers has weakened internal labor markets and is closing off opportunities for job security and advancement that, particularly for women, have only recently become available.[15]

Joining the Part-Time Workforce

Why do people seek or accept part-time jobs? What conditions make part-time employment an attractive option or the least undesirable alternative? Are there differences between women and men in their reasons for working part-time?

Generally, people work part-time because they want to, because their hours have been reduced due to slack work, or because they cannot find other suitable employment. Numerous studies of women who are employed part-time have documented the primacy of child care and household responsibilities in their decisions to work part-time.[16] My interviews with part-time workers support such findings. As might be expected, child care and household responsibilities do not figure prominently in men's decisions to work part-time. As the rates of voluntary and involuntary part-time employment reported in Table 5 show, men are less likely than women to want to work part-time.

Most people assume that women who choose part-time employment to accommodate child care and household responsibilities do so voluntarily. It is debatable, however, whether such women's decisions really constitute voluntary part-time employment. In a society that offers few alternatives to women who want or need to be employed and must tend to the home, there is an identifiable element of coercion in women's selection of part-time jobs.

About half of the part-time workers I spoke with actively sought to work part-time and most of them did so because they were also the primary caregivers of young children. Elizabeth Morgan was fairly typical of the women I spoke with who sought part-time employment upon becoming a mother. Elizabeth had two children when we spoke, a two-year-old daughter and an infant son who was just four months old. She worked full-time for five years before she began working part-time, and she sought to convert her job to part-time when she became pregnant with her first child. She did not actually obtain the reduction in her work hours that she wanted until a few months after that child was born.

Elizabeth was a clerical worker in state government. Technically, her wages were paid by a federal grant awarded to her supervisor who directed a special project for vision and hearing-impaired children. Elizabeth's opportunity to work part-time came when the grant monies were cut and the scope of the project was reduced from seven states to just one. With less work to do and fewer funds to pay workers, Elizabeth's supervisor agreed to reduce Elizabeth's hours—after she had spent a year "constantly pleading" to work part-time.

Lisa Adatto also sought to work part-time when her first child was born. That was seven years before I met her, and since that time she had given birth to a second child who was four years old when we spoke. Lisa planned to continue working part-time until her youngest child started school. By that time Lisa would complete her master's degree in nursing, a degree that she had been working on for two and a half years. Lisa was employed full-time for several years, first as a staff nurse, then as a nurse clinician and diabetes educator, before converting to part-time.

While many women who work part-time do so to balance employment and family responsibilities, others do so for other reasons. Helen Ferguson, for example, needed a better job. What she found was a second job. She had been employed full-time for ten years as a clerical worker at a collection agency. This job paid $4.75 an hour. Upon her divorce a few years before we met, Helen needed a job that paid a higher wage with better health insurance benefits and a retirement plan to support herself and her sixteen-year-old son. At first she looked for a full-time job. Finding none, she settled for a part-time job at a local retail store. Her part-time job paid $4.20 an hour, but the number of hours she worked varied from week to week. Some weeks she worked as few as eight hours; other weeks she worked as many as twenty hours in addition to her forty-hour, full-time job. Helen was still looking for that full-time job with higher pay and better benefits when I interviewed her.

None of the men I spoke with who were employed part-time sought part-time employment to accommodate household responsibilities. Nor had they actively sought part-time employment. Instead, they sought a particular kind of work and what they landed was a job they wanted but at part-time hours and pay. Joe Tedrich's case illustrates this point.

Joe's part-time job was one piece in the larger jigsaw puzzle of what he hoped would be a successful career. He was a sales clerk at a self-service retail store, part of a chain that employed his parents. He helped customers find merchandise, answered customers' questions, rang up their purchases, ordered merchandise for his department, and stocked shelves. Joe was a twenty-four-year-old high school graduate with three years' experience in this position. He hoped to move into management in the company and hoped his in-store experience and his good name—thanks to his parents' good reputations—would give him a competitive edge over other applicants for managerial positions.

Joe took this part-time job because it was his entree to the company. Like many retail companies today, the firm hires few full-time employees "off the street" unless they are hired into management. Without a business degree or managerial experience, Joe was not qualified to be hired directly into management. While he worked part-time gaining in-store experience, Joe attended college to earn a degree in business administration. When he perceived that the time was right, Joe planned to apply to become a management trainee. Joe could have been hired into a full-time clerk position that was vacant in his department, but he did not want to convey the wrong message to his employer. If he became a full-time clerk, he reasoned, his superiors would think he was content to be a clerk. Since he aspired to district-level management, Joe planned to continue to work part-time until he got his chance to become a full-time management trainee. Then he would become one of the company's "dogs," as he put it, doing whatever his superiors want him to do when they want it done. He anticipated that they would call him on a moment's notice, perhaps late at night, to work where he is needed, in different departments throughout the store, in a test of his commitment and loyalty to the company. Joe had resigned himself to this fate believing that in the end his dutiful servility would pay off in the form of a department of his own to manage, a regular 8:00 AM–4:00 PM or 9:00 AM–5:00 PM, full-time schedule, some semblance of autonomy as a store-level manager, and a stepping stone to mid-level management at the company's district headquarters.

As the cases discussed above illustrate, people work at part-time jobs for various reasons. Many women work part-time to balance paid work and child care. Teenagers and the elderly often work at part-time jobs to support themselves through school or to have an active role in the community. Some people work part-time to supplement their income from an inadequate full-time job. Others select part-time employment to gain experience in a field related to their career goals. While many individuals work part-time by choice, others do so because their hours have been cut or because they could not find a full-time job.

What effect does part-time employment have on overall quality of life? Does working part-time enhance or curb personal autonomy? Are there particular conditions under which part-time employment enhances autonomy and others that combine with part-time work to curb autonomy? Are there gender differences? These are the questions I will explore below in an analysis of part-time workers' work schedules and their use of time off the job.

Irregular Work Schedules

Most (about two-thirds) of the part-time workers I spoke with had irregular work schedules. That means they did not work the same hours every day or every week. Their hours fluctuated on a daily and weekly basis most often in response to business conditions. Not only did the timing of their work hours vary from day to day or week to week, but the total number of hours they worked on a weekly basis varied. Most of these individuals worked in jobs in the retail trade industry, and the irregularity of their work schedules reflects conditions in that industry. Only one individual I spoke with who worked an irregular schedule did not work in the retail trade industry. As a nurse/educator in the health care industry, her hours were essentially the same from week to week with minor fluctuations on certain days of the week when she saw patients. But because she made her own appointments with patients, she controlled the fluctuations in her work schedule, unlike most of the part-time workers in retail trade.

Work schedule variability is a fact of life for many employees in retail trade. Retail sales are elastic, fluctuating, depending on the particular industry, on a daily, weekly, monthly, and seasonal basis. Retail sales also fluctuate in relationship to holidays. Sales volume may rise and fall storewide and on a departmental basis. It is this inherent variability of retail sales that leads retailers to employ part-time workers whose hours can be scheduled in anticipation of these fluctuations. Such variability creates highly irregular work schedules for part-time employees in the retail sector.

A summary of the work schedules of three individuals I spoke with will illustrate the irregularity of work schedules in retail trade. Joe Tedrich, the young clerk I mentioned above, usually worked between thirty and forty hours a week although he was not scheduled for that many hours. He was usually scheduled for twenty-seven hours. Because Joe had the most seniority of the part-time clerks in his department, his supervisor was required to give him more hours than the other part-time clerks. Joe acquired the hours that he worked in excess of twenty-seven by volunteering to work in other departments that needed additional staff.

Joe's actual work schedule varied quite a lot from day to day and week to week and also depended to some extent on the schedules of the full-time clerks in his department. Sometimes Joe worked during the morning and afternoon; other times he worked during the afternoon and evening. He was more likely to work evenings during the week and days on the weekend because the full-time clerks with higher seniority tended to work days during the week. He often "opened" on Saturday and Sunday when the full-time clerk who was responsible for opening during the week was off, i.e., Joe started work at 7:00 AM and stayed until 3:00 PM.

Helen Ferguson, whose part-time job was a second job, worked anywhere from eight to twenty hours in a week. Her supervisor made her schedule at least three weeks in advance, giving Helen enough time to swap work hours with another employee if necessary. Helen could ensure that she was not scheduled for a particular day or certain hours by notifying her supervisor before she made the schedule. Because she worked from 8:00 AM to 5:00 PM Monday through Friday at her full-time job, Helen was only available to work in the evenings and on weekends at her part-time job.

Diane Howe was one of two tailors in the small alterations department of a large retail store. The other tailor worked full-time. Although Diane was hired to work part-time, she had worked full-time for several weeks before we spoke. The number of requests for alterations had been sufficiently large that she had been asked to work extra hours. She would return to working less than thirty hours per week when that demand dropped off.

When I interviewed her, Diane was working from 7:30 AM to 4:00 PM, Monday through Friday. If she missed a day during the week, she could make it up by working on the weekend. When she worked a part-time schedule, Diane worked fewer days each week.

Diane's case demonstrates that employers will increase part-time workers' hours to forty when the work load justifies doing so. Many part-time workers willingly accept the extra hours because they earn extra money. Their temporary shift to full-time hours, however, does not elevate them to full-time status. Therefore, their hourly rate remains at the part-time rate, and they only receive the benefits, if any, offered to part-time workers. And when the work load slackens, they will return to part-time hours. This case further illustrates the advantages of flexibility for employers who utilize part-time workers. Rather than hiring additional staff to meet the increased work load, employers temporarily increase part-time workers' hours, readily cutting back when the work load decreases.

As these cases illustrate, part-time workers' schedules vary on a daily and weekly basis, particularly if they are employed in the retail trade industry, and they also vary from one worker to another. How do irregular schedules of the sort I have just described affect workers' use of time off the job? To what extent do irregular schedules curb personal autonomy? Are there conditions under which personal autonomy is enhanced despite irregular schedules?

Irregular Work Schedules and Time Off the Job

Irregular work schedules, particularly when workers do not control them, make time unpredictable, and because someone else, usually a supervisor, controls the work schedule, prediction becomes an exercise in mind reading. Personal time management is difficult for persons with irregular work schedules over which they have little control, and this is reflected in how they use, or do not use, their time off the job.

The best illustration of the way in which irregular schedules can curb personal autonomy when workers have little control over their work schedules is the case of Lynn Karpinski. Lynn worked an irregular schedule as a part-time clerk at a discount department store. Lynn took this job because it was the best one offered to her. She looked for full-time employment, but she was considered only for part-time jobs. This one offered benefits, making it more attractive than the others that had been offered to her.

The irregularity of Lynn's schedule, and the fact that she had little control over it, made it difficult for her to plan off-the-job activities. Because her hourly rate was relatively low, although not as low as it would have been had she worked at a nonunion store, Lynn worked as many hours as she could to begin to make a living wage. Lynn was young—a high school graduate of two years—and lived with her parents who covered many of her living expenses, but these circumstances perpetuated Lynn's dependence on her parents. Her inadequate employment precluded her establishing her own independent life.

Lynn's responsibilities at the store included helping customers, straightening the department, and stocking shelves. During the pre-holiday season of October to December, two months before I spoke with her, she worked forty-eight-hour weeks. Two months later she was working just fifteen hours a week, the minimum guaranteed to part-time workers under the collective bargaining agreement. Lynn wanted more hours, but it was a slow season at the store and the hours just were not available. Lynn also had less than one year seniority, and employees in her department with more seniority received additional hours when they became available. Sometimes Lynn acquired additional hours in another department, but when business was generally slow even that was not an option.

Lynn's hours and schedule varied considerably over a period of several weeks. When I asked Lynn if she could give me a sense of her typical workweek, she could not, saying she had no typical workweek. Each week was up for grabs, and she learned how many hours she would work and at what times when her schedule was posted by her supervisor each Thursday. Lynn could request particular days off when she needed them, though she was reluctant to do so because her seniority was so low. She did not want to give her supervisor the impression that she did not want to work. For that reason, and because she wanted more hours, Lynn was "always available."

Lynn spent her time off the job at home, usually doing household work and helping her mother who had returned to school. She avoided activities that cost money because she had little discretionary income to spend. She wanted to volunteer to work with the United Way, but she could not commit herself because her work schedule was so unpredictable. Because she sought to be available whenever her employer might need her, she avoided undertaking activities that she could not easily abandon.

Lynn was in a bind, but she was strategically calculating a way out. She was not at all satisfied with her job, or her lifestyle, which had motivated her to consider going away to college in the hope of preparing herself for more secure, better-paying employment. But she would look for another part-time job to support herself through school. What Lynn had been experiencing as a disadvantage of part-time employment, the irregularity of work and work schedules, would become advantageous when she began college. Because part-time employment is flexible, she would be able to arrange work hours around her classes.

The problems of unpredictability associated with irregular work schedules disappear when the worker controls his or her schedule. Tessa James was a teacher in her late twenties who also worked part-time at a large retail store. She had worked part-time for this chain retailer for nine years, working her way up from sales clerk to sales supervisor. She had taken the job as a sales clerk while she was still a college student. With three years' experience, she was promoted to sales supervisor. Most of her responsibilities remained the same as those she had had as a sales clerk; she still helped customers make their purchases. But as a sales supervisor she had one area of responsibility that differed greatly from that of the clerks; she now made the work schedule for all workers in her department, including herself.

As a sales clerk, Tessa's work schedule was always made by a supervisor. Most supervisors accommodated her class schedule and her requests to work only in the evening and on weekends. One supervisor, however, in Tessa's view, seemed to deliberately avoid giving her the times off that she needed, apparently just to aggravate her. This meant that occasionally Tessa would have to miss classes. Once Tessa started her teaching job, however, she could not miss school to work at her part-time retail job. Many individuals would have quit the part-time job once they entered the career for which they had prepared. Because she had become the sales supervisor with responsibility for scheduling, Tessa did not have to make this choice. She worked at her teaching job during the day and supplemented her income by working at her part-time retail job in the evening and on weekends. With nine years, she was just one year away from being vested with her retail employer. After ten years, her retirement benefit would increase tenfold. When I spoke with her, the prospect of being vested is what motivated Tessa to keep her part-time job. The fact that she controlled her part-time work schedule made it easy for her to arrange her part-time job around her full-time teaching responsibilities. This was also a factor in her decision to return to graduate school. She could work on an advanced degree without giving up her income from her part-time job because she could arrange the hours she would spend at her retail job around her teaching responsibilities and graduate classes.

Irregular work schedules associated with part-time employment enhance or impede workers' personal autonomy depending upon the extent to which workers can control their work schedules. Irregular work schedules are a fact of life for many part-time workers, particularly those employed in retail trade, because employers use flexible scheduling to respond to business fluctuations. Workers with irregular schedules not subject to their control often find that the unpredictability of their work schedule interferes with their use of time off the job. Workers with irregular schedules that they control obviously do not have this problem. They can strike a better balance of employment and off-the-job activities.

Regular Work Schedules

While most of the part-time workers I interviewed had irregular work schedules, three had regular schedules. It is noteworthy that these individuals did not work in retail trade. They had jobs in the health care industry and the public sector. One woman, a clerical worker in state government, worked from 7:30 AM to 4:00 PM on Tuesdays, Wednesdays, and alternating Thursdays. She determined this schedule herself with the approval of her supervisor. Another woman, a clerical worker in a hospital, worked from 8:30 AM to 2:30 PM Monday through Thursday each week. She also determined this schedule with supervisory approval. She had changed her schedule three times since starting to work part-time to accommodate changes in her daughter's day-care arrangements. One man was a gardener who worked from 7:00 AM until 3:30 PM Monday through Friday from 1 April until 31 October, a schedule set by the municipality that employed him.

What effect do regular work schedules have on part-time workers' use of time off the job? Are there important differences among those who control their schedule and those who do not?

Regular Work Schedules and Time Off the Job

The problems associated with unpredictable work schedules, as illustrated above in the cases of those with irregular work schedules who had little control over them, may be overcome when the work schedule is regular, even if the worker has little control over the schedule. Regular schedules enhance predictability and planning despite workers' inability to control the work schedule.

Mark Putnam was a municipal gardener who worked seasonally under a schedule set by the city. He worked a forty-hour week, from 7:00 AM to 3:30 PM Monday through Friday, from 1 April to 31 October each year. While overtime was occasionally an option—Mark's seniority was too low for it to be offered to him often—Mark had no interest in working overtime. During the off-season, he collected unemployment insurance.

Mark took this job because he liked the work, but he had ambivalent feelings about being seasonally employed. His Protestant middle-class upbringing, as he characterized it, "says no, no, no, you ought to be working a full-time job." On the other hand, he enjoyed being off during the winter. It gave him time for activities that he ordinarily did not have time for, and it gave him "intellectual free time." For Mark, regular, year-round, full-time employment would have been physically and emotionally detrimental.

Mark's job was physically demanding. He was a member of the landscape crew, which tended the city's public gardens, parks, and golf courses. "Outdoor housecleaning," Mark called it. He described himself as someone who needed to be outdoors, who could not deal with being indoors all the time, who wanted to be in contact with the natural world. He "feels better" when he spends time outdoors.

But by the end of the season, Mark's work becomes tiring and monotonous. During the off-season he shifts his attention to less demanding manual labor and more demanding intellectual work. He takes art classes to study color; he offers consultation to local businesses planning landscapes; he participates in the city's beautification program; and he attends seminars on political issues that interest him. The off-season is an opportunity to fulfill autonomous needs through self-employment and community service.

Mark was thirty-eight years old and unmarried when we spoke, although he and his domestic partner planned to marry soon thereafter. Leslie was a midwife, so her work rhythm coincided with her clients' cycles of pregnancy and childbirth. During the prenatal period, she offered counseling, training, and support to her clients. At the time of labor and delivery, she offered in-hospital labor support. Leslie had some control over scheduling prenatal counseling and training, but she had to respond to her clients' biological rhythms during labor and delivery. Mark said there are times when Leslie is out of the house for two or three full days during a client's critical labor and delivery period. Because Leslie's time was usually under her control, she assumed most of the responsibility for household work during the spring and summer when Mark worked his forty-hour weeks. During Mark's off-season, however, he assumes the lion's share of household work in a trade-off with Leslie.

Mark achieved a balance of physical and mental activity in his life, and therefore a sense of autonomy, not because he controlled his work schedule but because his schedule was regular and predictable and because it afforded him a large quantity of unobligated time. Because he drew unemployment benefits in the off-season, he existed at a level of material comfort that freed him from the necessity to seek additional employment.

Sarah Martin achieved a similar sense of autonomy from her part-time job, in large measure because she controlled her work schedule. Sarah worked part-time as a secretary at a private hospital. Her duties varied a lot because she worked on several different projects over the course of a year. Her regular duties included transcribing dictation from a machine, typing memos, and replacing the administrative secretary when she was absent. In addition, Sarah inventoried patient education materials and scheduled interviews with prospective residents. Sarah had just completed her first year in this position after transferring from another office where she had worked full-time for seven years.

Sarah worked twenty-four hours each week, six hours a day Monday through Thursday. At first she worked from noon until 4:00 PM Monday through Friday, then 8:00 AM to 1:00 PM Monday through Friday. Shortly before we spoke she had changed her schedule to 8:30 AM to 2:30 PM Monday through Thursday because that schedule meshed best with her daughter's day-care arrangements. The quality of Sarah's time with her daughter had also improved since Sarah changed her work schedule to 8:30 AM to 2:30 PM. As she explained to me,

> When I used to work from 8:00 to 1:00 I wouldn't pick my daughter up until 1:30, and at that point in the day she wouldn't have had her nap. She'd be pretty wound up when I'd get her home, and I'd struggle with her to get her down for her nap. Before you'd know it, it'd be 4:00. So now she pretty much gets

her nap out of the way by the time I pick her up. So we do things together. Sometimes we go shopping. We've been working with her alphabet, reading, drawing, trying to teach her how to write her letters, things like that.

Sarah Martin's experience of part-time employment illustrates the extent to which she can be involved in her daughter's life despite employment outside the home. She satisfies her desires for employment, she fulfills her expectations of herself as a mother, and she strikes an optimum balance between these two spheres of activity because she controls her work schedule.[17]

Part-time employment helps mothers integrate paid employment and child care, however, it should not be assumed that part-time employment maximizes women's personal autonomy. Women's personal autonomy may go beyond facilitating child care and household responsibilities to free time for recreation, community service, and other activities. Some women I spoke with had difficulty finding time for recreation despite the reduction in time devoted to their jobs and the ability to control their work schedule. This is the case for Elizabeth Morgan, the part-time clerical worker in state government I mentioned above. She had been married to an electrician for six years. They had two small children, ages two years and four months. Elizabeth went to the office two or three days each week, working from 7:30 AM to 4:00 PM each day. Her working days began at 5:15 AM so she had enough time to nurse her infant daughter, get dressed to go to the office, and get her children ready to go to their caretaker's house. Elizabeth took her children to the caretaker's on her way to the office and picked them up on her way home.

Elizabeth said she had "a lot of free time" because she works less than full-time. But she spends most of that "free" time around the house, playing with and enjoying her children. She bakes too, because that is something she likes to do, and occasionally she visits her mother who lives nearby or friends who also are employed part-time. One night each weekend Elizabeth and her husband go out on a "date" and leave their children with a caretaker. Elizabeth thinks being away from the children occasionally is good for her relationship with her husband.

Despite all of her "free time," Elizabeth yearned for more time for herself. "I think I should get away more," Elizabeth confided in me. "Probably a few days I'd like to get a sitter and just go and have time by myself," she explained. Elizabeth felt a little guilty that she desired time for herself, believing she had time for herself when she was at the office. Yet that time at the office was not quite what she had in mind when she said she wanted time for herself. Because she worked part-time, Elizabeth thought she should be at home with her children during her time off. But she resented the fact that she shouldered all of the responsibility for household work and child care. Elizabeth described her husband as a man who was "not a real big help" around the house or with the children. When she was home, he deferred to her in these areas. Elizabeth's husband was aware of the inequity in their division of labor, but he did little to remedy the problem. In his mind, the solution was for Elizabeth to leave the house more often, perhaps in the evening when he is at home, thereby "sticking" him with the responsibility to mind their children.

Elizabeth was in a catch-22. She enjoyed being home with her children, but she resented having all of the responsibility for their care. She wanted her husband to want to be as involved in their care as she was. In their interpersonal struggle over free time, Elizabeth lost because her husband abdicated his participation in household work and child care. If he had carried more of the responsibility, Elizabeth could carry less, giving her more time for herself. As it was, she found time for herself at the office or at home when her other responsibilities were "over," usually late at night, just before bedtime. Men, in Elizabeth's view, had free time whenever they wanted it. Such was the injustice Elizabeth experienced in her household routine despite the fact that she worked part-time and determined her own work schedule. For Elizabeth, and many women like her, it is not the work schedule that inhibits her participation in recreational activities. An argument might be made that her children are the obstacle she must overcome, but closer examination reveals that Elizabeth's husband's lack of participation in child care, his deference to his wife in this sphere of activity, and Elizabeth's own ideology of motherhood combine to prevent Elizabeth from pursuing a self-determined recreational activity. Elizabeth's experience points to the stranglehold of gender which exists despite women's part-time work schedules. Circumstances such as these raise doubts about the potential for greater autonomy for women under conditions of reduced work, even when they control their own work schedule.

Summary and Conclusion

As this chapter has documented, part-time employment is on the rise in the United States. The majority of individuals who work part-time do so voluntarily; this is particularly true of women who work part-time to integrate wage work and household responsibilities. I suggested, however, that in the absence of employment alternatives for women with household responsibilities who also want or need a wage-paying job, part-time employment may not be entirely voluntary. Women with children may feel they have no choice but to work part-time.

The recent growth in part-time employment in the United States is accounted for in large part by the increase in involuntary part-time employment. As employers hire greater numbers of part-time workers to reduce labor costs and maximize flexibility in the scheduling of staff, increasing numbers of individuals who prefer full-time employment are able only to find part-time jobs.

My interviews with part-time workers substantiated many of the already published claims regarding part-time employment. These data revealed that individuals work part-time for myriad reasons: to accommodate child care responsibilities; to integrate job and school; to get work experience in a chosen field; because work is slack; and because no full-time job was available.

This chapter also explored the effects of part-time employment on personal autonomy and the quality of life. I argued that the nature of the work schedule and the level of income interact with a complex of other factors (like ability to control the schedule, marital status or household structure, presence and ages of children, as well as gender of the part-time worker) to influence the experience of part-time employment. Irregular schedules not controlled by the worker inhibit the ability to plan and make commitments, thereby limiting the worker to activities that can be undertaken spontaneously. Regular schedules not controlled by the worker solve this problem of unpredictability, but such schedules may interfere with off-the-job activities because the worker cannot determine the timing of his or her job to achieve a better fit with other activities. Schedules controlled by the worker, whether they are regular or irregular, maximize the individual's ability to integrate employment with other activities. The relatively low income associated with most part-time jobs, however, means individuals have little discretionary income to use for off-the-job activities unless there is supplementary financial support. Therefore, part-time workers may have time to pursue a variety of off-the-job activities, but their lack of discretionary income may limit their choices. Depending upon this complex of factors, individuals may experience part-time employment as enriching or impoverishing. To the extent that it facilitates participation in a variety of activities without financial hardship, it is enriching. To the extent that it may contribute to the social isolation of workers, either because the work schedule is unpredictable or because earnings are inadequate or both, part-time employment is impoverishing.

Women who are employed part-time to accommodate child care responsibilities may find they have little free time despite their part-time employment. Their child care responsibilities may be sufficiently burdensome to preclude their participation in other activities. Part-time work for many women is an accommodation to dual spheres of responsibility. In this sense, reduced work reinforces, rather than challenges, conventional definitions of gender and the gender division of labor. Women's personal autonomy, therefore, may not be enhanced by part-time employment despite their ability to better integrate wage work and household responsibilities.

Chapter Five

The Temporaries

Temporary employees are an increasingly significant subgroup of all of those who are employed less than full-time. The temporary help supply (THS) industry in the United States boomed during the 1980s. In 1956 there were approximately twenty thousand employees in the THS industry. More recently it has been estimated that two to three million workers are employed as temporaries at some time during each year, often for only a few hours, but more frequently for several days over a period of three or four months.[1] Temporaries comprised about 2 percent of the U.S. labor force in the early 1980s, but that figure was expected to triple by the early 1990s.[2] In the two-year period from November 1982 to November 1984 the number of employees in the THS industry grew 70 percent.[3] The temporary help supply industry was the third fastest growing industry in the United States in the early 1980s, with 90 percent of businesses and practically all of the Fortune 500 companies using temporaries on a regular basis.[4] The industry grew twice as fast as the gross national product during the 1970s and the first half of the 1980s, and faster than the computer equipment industry, to a payroll of $5.5 billion in 1984. This compares to a payroll of $431 million just thirteen years earlier.[5]

In the early 1970s, most temporaries were employed as clerical workers, and most of them were young women.[6] More recently, it has been estimated that 65 percent of temporary employment is in clerical work, 30 percent is in manual labor, and 5 percent is in professional and technical work.[7] There also has been considerable growth in temporary employment in the health care industry, particularly among registered and licensed practical nurses and other health care professionals and technicians.[8]

With the exception of temporaries hired directly by a company or organization, temporaries are employees of the THS company, not the organization where they hold a placement. The THS company pays the employees' wages and any benefits it provides. Temporary help supply companies provide their employees with legally required benefits, such as social security, workers' compensation, and unemployment insurance, but temporaries may be expected to accumulate as many as twelve hundred or fifteen hundred hours to qualify for sick pay, holiday pay, health insurance, or other benefits common in industry.[9] Once they qualify, they may also have to work a minimum number of hours per month, each month, to continue to be eligible for such benefits. The actual rate of pay for temporary workers may be the same as, slightly lower, or higher than that of regular employees doing the same work.[10]

Temporary help supply companies are labor brokers who charge employers a fee for using their employees. For most organizations, paying this fee represents a cost savings over hiring workers directly. If the organization were to hire a new employee directly, it likely would have to pay wages and benefits far in excess of the fee paid to the THS company. Organizations may also find it advantageous to use a THS company's employees, rather than hire temporaries directly, because the THS company absorbs the costs of recruitment and training that the organization would otherwise have to pay. More importantly, however, an organization's cost savings come principally in its ability to readily terminate temporaries when need for their labor subsides. Hired directly by an employer or through a THS company, temporaries often are hired for special projects, to replace workers on vacation or leave, or for peak demand periods that occur during an upturn in the business cycle. When the project ends, the regular employee returns, or business turns downward, temporaries are easily terminated. The use of temporary workers, alone or in combination with part-time workers, allows managers to trim their permanent, full-time work force. Such management efforts to build a flexible, lean work force have led to the expansion of temporary employment for reasons similar to that of part-time employment. Temporary employees, like part-time workers, help reduce an organization's labor costs.

Seeking Temporary Employment

Why do individuals seek and accept temporary jobs? Generally, they seek temporary employment for reasons similar to those that motivate individuals who seek part-time employment. Either they do not want or cannot find permanent, full-time employment. Notably, however, none of the temporaries I spoke with sought temporary employment in order to integrate wage work with child care. As I will demonstrate below, temporary employment is far too unpredictable to integrate it with child care.

Some individuals like the variety associated with temporary employment. Because temporaries often move among a number of different placements, they experience variation in their work responsibilities and work environments that most regularly employed people do not experience. Such variety is especially attractive to individuals with relatively few skills because variety relieves boredom.[11]

Many people like temporary employment because it gives them some control over when and where they work. When applying for temporary employment, individuals can specify when they are available, whether they want full-time or part-time hours, and the type of job or jobs they are willing or able to perform. When the THS company calls them with a placement offer, temporaries can choose to accept or reject the offer. One temporary I spoke with had learned something of the reputations of various employers, and when she received offers of placements with employers whose reputations were particularly negative she declined. Of course, only temporaries with some degree of financial security can afford to reject offers of employment, no matter what the reputation of the employer. Financially secure or not, however, temporary employees exercise this discretion with caution so as not to convey to the THS company a general unwillingness to work.

Some people work as temporaries indefinitely because they like the arrangement for the sorts of reasons just mentioned.[12] Others use temporary employment as a transition to other occupational or personal pursuits. The interviews I conducted with temporaries support these claims, but I also met temporaries who appeared to be stuck in temporary jobs. They had chosen temporary employment as a last resort, discouraged that they could not find steady, full-time work, and they remained employed as temporaries because they continued to be unable to find anything else and harbored some hope that their temporary job might be offered to them permanently. This phenomenon of involuntary temporary employment points again to the structural shifts occurring in the nation's economy and the related transformations of the nation's occupational structure. Opportunities for regular, full-time employment are shrinking as employers reduce the size of their full-time work force. When individuals want a full-time job and cannot find one, they face unpleasant alternatives. If they want to avoid unemployment, they have little choice but to take a part-time or temporary job since those sectors of the labor market are growing rapidly.

Students like temporary employment because it offers them flexibility comparable to part-time employment but perhaps at higher levels of pay. Two students with whom I spoke had selected temporary employment for these reasons. They worked as full-time temporaries during the summer, doing clerical work in state government, and earned $5.00 an hour. This rate of pay was well above the minimum wage at the time, making temporary clerical work more attractive to these students than work at a fast-food restaurant, for example. They preferred to work as many hours as possible during the summer, earning as much money as possible, and quitting when school resumed in the fall to devote their energies to their studies during the academic year.

Another student I spoke with, however, pieced together year-round employment through a combination of part-time and temporary jobs. She worked from eighteen to twenty-two hours a week at her part-time job at a fast food restaurant (earning $3.35 an hour) and twelve hours a week at her temporary clerical job at a hospital (earning $4.75 an hour). She was paying her own tuition in addition to her living expenses, and neither job paid enough by itself to support her.

Two other people I spoke with preferred temporary employment for the flexibility and autonomy it can provide. Peggy Needham was the primary breadwinner in her household while her husband attended graduate school full-time. Initially Peggy wanted a permanent, full-time job. Upon moving to a new community when her husband started school, Peggy became a temporary to tide them over until she could find a permanent, full-time job. After six months of steady, full-time work as a temporary, Peggy found a permanent, full-time job as an office manager in a career consulting firm. But the organization was managed poorly, she thought, so Peggy left that company within six months. Peggy returned to the THS company that had employed her previously. This time, however, it took them five weeks to find a placement for her, and they could only come up with one that would last one week. Peggy felt betrayed. "They weren't there for me," she told me, characterizing the experience as "tragic"" and one that should have but did not correct for the loss of self-confidence she suffered at the career consulting firm. Peggy sought out another THS company, which she found to be "very receptive" and "very friendly." "They recognized my talents right off," she explained, "and they were ready to put me right on the job." Peggy worked steadily for three months at a full-time temporary clerical job prior to my interview with her. Her placement would be terminated in another month, however, when her predecessor returned from maternity leave. Peggy planned to seek another temporary placement and continue working as a temporary until her husband finished his degree within the next year. Peggy anticipated that they would relocate then, and she reasoned that it would be easier for her to quit a temporary job. She also believed an employer would not hire her for a permanent, full-time job knowing that she intended to quit in less than a year.

Karen Lyons was a youth pastor's wife who sought part-time temporary employment to "fill in my days." She devoted a lot of evenings and weekends to church activities, which were quite important to her, but had too much free time during the week. She and her husband had no children, although they hoped to in the not-too-distant future. Because they planned to start a family soon and Karen intended to stay home with their children, she did not want a permanent job. Her part-time temporary job used up some of her free time without interfering with her religious activities, and it would be easy to quit when her family responsibilities increased.

About half of the temporaries I spoke with were using temporary employment as a transition to a regular, full-time job, or so they hoped. One twenty-two-year-old woman whom I will call Terry had had difficulty finding a full-time job after completing two quarters at a local community college. Her specialty was data entry, but employers repeatedly told her she did not have enough experience for the positions they advertised. To gain experience and have time to continue her search for a full-time job, Terry signed up with a THS company. The temporary placements would give her the additional experience employers wanted, she thought, and she could use her time between placements to apply for permanent, full-time jobs.

Unfortunately, things were not working out quite the way Terry had hoped. In the first three months after joining the temporary work force, she had had two brief placements. A job stuffing envelopes lasted two and a half weeks, and one processing insurance premium payments lasted two days. And she still had no promising leads on a regular, full-time job.

Meg Riley, on the other hand, was having quite a different experience of temporary employment when I met her. Meg was a thirty-three-year-old woman of exceptional education and skill. She had a master's degree in economics and several credits toward the Ph.D. She had had five different placements in the six months she had been a temporary employee. She had consistently worked full-time weeks, earning the equivalent of thirteen thousand dollars in annual income.

After five months, she had accumulated enough hours to be eligible for small health and life insurance packages through the THS company. Her placement at the time I spoke with her, which she had had for two months, was a clerical job at a large university. She had just accepted an offer to take this job permanently for an annual salary of twenty thousand dollars and employer-provided benefits.

With her level of education, why did Meg Riley sign up for temporary employment? She had started her own consulting company after working for four years as a vice-president for research, earning forty-two thousand dollars a year, for another consulting company. Management problems that developed in that company led Meg to strike out on her own. In time the burden of running her own company became overwhelming. She spent "considerable time" traveling, making sales calls, meeting people, and attending meetings in what many might see as an exciting whirlwind of activity to drum up business. Meg devoted so much time and energy to finding clients that she had little time for research and writing, the work that she enjoys. Not a risk taker by nature, Meg had two options: go deeper into debt to keep her company afloat or quit and find another job in which she could do the kind of work that she likes. She chose the latter. Knowing it could take a while to locate a job to match her skills and education, Meg chose temporary employment to provide an income in the interim. The permanent, full-time job she had just accepted when I spoke with her was not her ideal job, but she took it with the understanding that her responsibilities could be reshaped within a year. Her job was not sufficiently challenging, but she saw potential for growth. She worked in a new administrative unit in the university, one that, she believed, could use her skills in public speaking, public relations, and research. Meg was optimistic that she could create a more stimulating job for herself, but if that did not work out at least she was "in" at the university. If more appealing jobs opened on campus, she would apply for them with confidence that she would have a competitive edge: Under the university's agreement with the clerical workers union, the university first must seek to hire from within.

THS companies are off-site personnel departments for employers who use them. The THS company tests, trains (in some instances), and screens job applicants, matching workers to the particular needs of employers. THS companies save employers money by providing this service. In the absence of this service, employers must employ more people to do this work for them. Usually temporary employees are just that—temporary. They fill a short-term need for extra staff, perhaps when a regular employee is on vacation or an employer is

engaged in a special project. For the employer, however, using temporaries is also an opportunity to scrutinize workers on the job. An
employer who needs to expand the permanent staff can select the
most desirable workers from among a group of temporaries who pass
through the workplace. Without expecting it or necessarily looking for
it, this is what happened to Meg Riley. It is difficult to know how
many temporaries are offered permanent jobs, but I suspect it is an
unusual outcome rather than the norm. Of the twelve temporaries I
spoke with, three had had such offers. Desperate individuals aware of
the fact that some temporary jobs become permanent will apply for
temporary work in their search for regular, full-time employment.
Workers quite obviously are disappointed when this happy scenario
does not occur.

Ed Pavlachak had applied for temporary work in the hopes of
landing a permanent, full-time job. He had worked two and a half
months in a temporary job unloading trucks when I met him. For ten
years, Ed had worked intermittently at a variety of jobs, unable to find
steady, full-time work after being fired from a job. He applied for temporary employment as a kind of last resort. He hoped his current
placement would be offered to him permanently and was encouraged
by the fact that two coworkers had been hired permanently after brief
periods of temporary service. His employer had not made him an
offer of permanent employment, however, nor had he hinted at the
prospect. Consequently, Ed faced an uncertain future.

Althea Bridges also pursued temporary employment as a last
resort, although she had come to like it for its autonomy and flexibility. Althea had worked on the assembly line at an automobile plant for
eleven months before she was laid off in November 1985. Althea
remained unemployed for about six months after she was laid off. For
a long time she believed she would be called back to the plant. After
her unemployment insurance benefits expired, however, and she had
not been called back, she conducted an extensive job search. Having
had no luck finding another job, Althea signed up for temporary
employment. That was about nine months before I met her. During
that nine months, Althea had worked thirty-seven hours a week each
week. She earned $4.15 an hour at a clerical job that she accepted only
because the THS company could not find anything else for her. Althea
had been a clerical worker for thirteen years before taking the job at
the auto plant, but she really did not like clerical work.

It had been almost a year and a half since Althea had been laid
off when I met her, and she had just about given up all hope that the
auto company would call her back to work. Her temporary job had

recently been offered to her as a permanent, full-time job. She weighed the advantages and disadvantages of full-time employment during our conversation, but she remained undecided about accepting the offer. Althea had grown to like temporary employment because she liked the option of taking Mondays off occasionally to have a long weekend with her husband. He was still employed at the auto plant where Althea had worked, earning $17.00 an hour as a reliever on the line. Many weeks he worked forty-eight hours. While Althea had experienced a 65 percent drop in her hourly wage when she went from her full-time job on the assembly line to her temporary clerical job, her husband's earnings remained strong and secure for the foreseeable future. For this reason Althea felt little pressure to have a regular, well-paying, full-time job.

In sum, individuals seek and accept temporary jobs for a variety of reasons. Some like the flexibility and autonomy associated with deciding when and where to work. Others use temporary employment as a stepping stone to other pursuits or to gain work experience. Still others turn to temporary employment as a more desirable alternative to unemployment, perhaps hoping a temporary job will be offered to them permanently.

We now have some understanding of why individuals work at temporary jobs, but how does temporary employment affect their quality of life? As I will explain below, the nature of the work schedule and levels of pay combine to enrich or impoverish temporary workers' overall quality of life.

Regular Work Schedules

Most of the twelve temporaries I spoke with had regular work schedules, although they had little control over their schedules beyond preferences they had specified on the application form. Most of the temporaries with regular schedules also worked full-time hours. They worked full-time because they wanted to; they wanted steady employment, and they sought to earn a living wage. They also anticipated that their placements were finite. Some were told when they accepted an offer that the placement would end at a certain time, perhaps within a few days, a few weeks, or several months. Others had been told their placements were indefinite, although because the job was temporary they expected the job to end at some point unless it was offered to them permanently. Those who had received offers of permanent employment, of course, had not been told to anticipate such an outcome when the temporary job was first extended to them. Therefore, most temporaries accept temporary jobs as they simultaneously prepare to be unemployed when the placement terminates. Anticipating unemployment of unknown longevity or a return to school upon termination of the temporary job, the full-time temporaries I met wanted to earn as much as they could during the time they were employed.

The temporary, full-time clerical workers had work schedules established by the offices where they held placements (for example, 8:00 AM to 5:00 PM or 8:00 AM to 4:30 PM Monday through Friday). One clerical worker, however, established her own schedule within the limits of the flexitime rules where she was placed. She worked from 7:30 AM to 4:00 PM Monday through Friday with options for overtime. The part-time temporary clerical workers I spoke with worked from 8:00 AM to 5:00 PM or from 1:00 PM to 5:00 PM three days a week. They had requested particular days during the week, or afternoons on certain days of the week, to mesh employment with other activities. The lone full-time temporary manual laborer I met worked from 7:00 AM to 3:30 PM Monday through Friday at a schedule set by his employer.

How do regular work schedules affect the use of time off the job among temporary workers? That is the question to which I now turn.

Regular Work Schedules and Time Off the Job

Like the part-time workers with regular work schedules discussed in chapter four, temporaries with regular work schedules have predictable schedules that facilitate planning off-the-job activities even when they do not control their work schedules. Most of the full-time temporaries I met, however, complained about time scarcity. Because they devoted as many weekly hours to a job as permanently employed full-time workers, they experienced shortages of free time as regular full-time workers often do. They complained of too much "free time" devoted to household responsibilities and too little time for recreational and social activities. This was especially true of the women I spoke with. But the temporaries also despaired of limited income. They had little discretionary income to spend on recreation and entertainment. Because their earnings barely stretched far enough to cover necessities and long-term employment was not assured, the temporaries were compelled to work as many hours as were available to them to earn as much money as possible. The exceptions were those with alternative sources of financial support, particularly two married women whose husbands were the primary earners in their households. With such alternative support, these women could maximize the flexiblity often touted to accompany temporary employment. In the absence of such alternative support, full-time temporaries remained subject to the tyranny of the forty-hour week.

Meg Riley, the temporary clerical worker with a master's degree in economics whom I mentioned above, had worked forty-hour weeks since taking her current placement two months before I met her. Although she had worked steadily and full-time, she had suffered a substantial loss of income since leaving the consulting firm where she was employed a few years earlier. She had gained free time since then, but her limited discretionary income prevented her from using that time in ways that she would have enjoyed.

When Meg was with the consulting firm, she worked eighty-five to ninety hours each week, often six or seven days each week. She had a large income but little free time. As she reflected on her lifestyle then, she characterized herself as "one-dimensional." "It was a major effort to schedule leisure activities," she told me. On any given work day, Meg awoke at 5:00 AM; ate breakfast, dressed, and walked her dog before leaving home; arrived at her office by 7:00 AM; returned home at 9:00 PM; prepared and ate dinner; washed her dishes; took her dog for his evening walk; read the newspaper before listening to the eleven o'clock news; and retired when the news program ended. Day after day she lived the same routine. "There was no time for talking to anyone, going anyplace, watching any movies, taking in any theatre, going to any concerts, reading any books, doing anything around the house, or anything else," she complained.

Meg worked somewhat fewer hours, fifty-five or sixty each week, for the brief period of time when she was self-employed after leaving the consulting firm and before joining the temporary work force, but her income was almost 50 percent less than what she had earned when she worked for the consulting firm. She lost employee benefits when she left the firm, so she had to purchase individual insurance policies when she was self-employed. The decrease in her income and the added expense of insurance limited her discretionary income. Previously, her principal recreational activity had been regular attendance at theatre performances, and she was a season ticket holder. As a self-employed person, she still went to the theatre, but only occasionally, and she could no longer afford to purchase season tickets although she had more time to attend performances. The economist lived the irony of the time/income tradeoff. Her free time increased, but her income decreased, so she had to find less costly recreational activities.

As a temporary, Meg's income had declined an additional 50 percent. While her forty-hour workweek limited her recreational activities somewhat, it was her lack of discretionary income that most curbed her options. As a temporary worker, she spent most of her time off the job "puttering" around the house. Despite fewer hours of work, her life had become one-dimensional again.

Ed Pavlachak, the full-time manual temporary, also spent most of his time off the job puttering around the house. Ed lived with his wife of twenty years, their three children, and a grandchild. He was one of three earners in the household; combined they earned less than twenty thousand dollars a year. Despite his wife's contribution of 50 percent of their combined income, Ed considered himself the primary breadwinner because he had been the sole breadwinner until a short time before I met him. Their daughter was employed full-time and managed her income separately from her parents', but she paid rent to live in their home with her daughter.

Money was a worrisome issue for Ed. The topic of insufficient income came up repeatedly throughout my conversation with him. Because his family had lived at or near the poverty level for many years, Ed worked as many hours as he could. He wanted to do wood-working in his time off the job, but he could not afford to purchase wood, tools, and the other supplies he needed to make something. So he puttered and watched television during his time off the job.

Meg Riley and Ed Pavalachak both had work-centered lives, but not by their own choice. They are not examples of "workaholics" building professional careers, because their jobs were not on a career path (although they hoped they would be). Their work-centered lives were a consequence of their low wages. To eke out a decent living, they had to work as much as they could. Their recreational choices, when they were off the job, were circumscribed by limited time and little discretionary income. Their low wages and the amount of time they devoted to their jobs combined to narrow the range of recreational activities they could realistically pursue.

Peggy Needham had similar complaints, but it was the lack of time rather than the lack of money that distressed her most. Prior to her temporary full-time job, Peggy had been employed part-time. When she worked part-time, and her husband worked full-time, she had time to help friends in addition to time to socialize with her husband, participate in church activities, and meet her household responsibilities. Once Peggy's husband enrolled in school full-time and she became the primary breadwinner with a temporary full-time job, Peggy did not have time to help friends in the ways she wanted to help them.

Peggy told me about a friend who was bedridden for the last seven weeks of her pregnancy. Peggy very much wanted to help her, but she could not be available in the afternoons when her friend most needed help. This is an instance when the responsibility of being a primary breadwinner came into conflict with Peggy's sense of herself as a person and as a woman. Peggy told me she found it important to "take time out for other people," and she perceived her inability to do so as an injustice created by her husband. If he were employed, she told me, she could take time off to help her friend. In other words, if he were the primary breadwinner, fulfilling men's normative family role, then she could be the kind of woman and friend that she wanted to be. But the rearrangement of earning responsibilities, albeit temporary, to which Peggy and her husband had agreed, effected a rearrangement of gender relations that Peggy found somewhat untenable. The source of Peggy's problem, however, which she failed to see, is a system of employment that is inflexible and does not permit workers, of either gender, to engage in the kind of helping behaviors that were so important to Peggy. In Peggy's view, it would have been a better arrangement if her husband worked full-time and she had time to help friends. But this is the traditional gender arrangement that has contributed to women's oppression since the inception of paid work. As primary nurturers of children, the aging, and the infirm, women have been distracted from and excluded from full participation in society. And traditional gender arrangements, as they have influenced the system of employment, have prevented men, or excused them, from doing nurturing and caring work (men who are employed in nurturing occupations are an obvious exception here). A more flexible and gender-egalitarian employment system would encourage such nurturing work by permitting workers to take time off to provide care and help to others, and it would encourage both women and men to do so.

As the social psychologist Charles Horton Cooley argued, the separation of self and other, or self and society as he put it, is a false dichotomy.[13] The extension of support and help to friends and kin or through more formally organized community services are sources of self-fulfillment to the extent that we derive pleasure and satisfaction from them, and they are products of self-expression in that our participation is an expression of our interests, needs, and desires. Therefore, connection to others is an element of self. Community service also enhances our sense of citizenship to the extent that our activities contribute to some sense of the common good. Historically, American women have played a critical role in civic life, although their role too often has been overlooked and undervalued. Through their participation in voluntary associations located between the public world of politics and employment and the private intimacy of family, women's politicized domesticity has spearheaded many of the important reform movements in American history.[14]

Religious activities are common channels for women's politicized domesticity, particularly in sects where the tradition of good works remains strong.[15] Karen Lyons, a part-time temporary, was a young woman whose orientation to public service grew from religious commitment and the support role she played alongside her husband, a youth minister. Karen devoted twenty-five to thirty hours each week to church activities. She belonged to several committees, attended prayer meetings a couple evenings a week, helped with a children's group on Monday nights, and spent most all day Sunday in services and meetings. Most of these activities were matters of personal choice, but Karen participated in a few because she believed it was her duty to do so as the youth minister's wife. Karen was the unpaid half of a two-person career.[16] As the youth minister's wife, she was expected to participate in certain church activities in a demonstration of support for her husband and the church. While the church could not reprimand her directly if she did not participate, her husband's career might suffer if he had what might appear to be an unsupportive wife.

Karen's religious activities were a part-time job in themselves, but they were the most important activities in her life when I spoke with her. Because she and her husband had not had children yet in their young marriage, Karen felt that she had extra time on her hands. To fill some of that time and supplement her husband's income, she sought part-time, temporary employment. She usually worked on Monday, Tuesday, and Thursday each week from 8:00 AM to 5:00 PM. Occasionally she worked on Wednesday or Friday if necessary. Karen negotiated the days she worked with her employer, but the eight-to-five schedule was firm. Her supervisors were flexible, Karen reported happily, in that she could trade Monday, for example, for another day during the week if she needed to.

Flexible Mondays and Fridays were important to Karen because occasionally she and her husband accompanied church youths on weekend trips. When they did that, Karen needed Friday to prepare for the trip and Monday to unpack and do laundry. Karen's obligations to her husband and the church required that she have a part-time job with flexible hours.

As noted above, even when workers have little control over their work schedules, regular work schedules have an important advantage over irregular schedules. Regular schedules enhance the ability to plan off-the-job activities and to follow through when commitments have been made. Workers know far in advance when they will have to be on the job, and this predictability facilitates planning and commitment to off-the-job activities. The number of work hours and their timing, however, may limit the array of off-the-job activities from which they may choose. Night workers, for example, who sleep during the day are barred from participating in activities that compose much of the fabric of social life because those activities occur during daytime hours. Persons who work forty-hour weeks may complain that they have little free time, especially if they have responsibilities that occupy much of their time off the job. Financial insecurity motivates people to work extra hours when the hours are available, thereby reducing their time off the job. Temporary employment and financial insecurity intersect in complex ways to influence time off the job. How do these factors influence the quality of life among temporaries who work intermittently? That is the question I take up next.

Intermittent Temporary Work

Three individuals had worked intermittently since applying for temporary employment, and they were between placements when I spoke with them. One man who preferred industrial work had applied for temporary jobs about a month before I spoke with him. He had worked two weeks performing janitorial services and one week doing automobile repair. It had been a week since his last placement ended when I met him. Another man had applied for temporary clerical work about six weeks previous to my interview with him. He had had four placements during that time, ranging in duration from six hours to three days, performing work such as stuffing envelopes and filing. One woman had applied for temporary clerical work four months before I met her. During that time she had had just two placements. The first was supposed to last three weeks but terminated a few days early when the work to be done had been completed. The second lasted two days. When I spoke with her, it had been more than a month since her last placement. The latter two cases were unemployed more than they were employed; they spent more time waiting for a job than actually working at one. Although the woman had turned down a few offers, the man told me that he was willing to do almost any kind of work that he was physically capable of performing.

Temporaries who are employed intermittently have little control over their work schedules. Most of the time they do not know whether or when they will have a job. They cannot anticipate when they will receive placement offers, nor can they anticipate the nature of those placements in terms of employer, location, pay, hours, and duration. Each of the intermittently employed temporaries I met had preferred full-time temporary jobs, but the THS company had had difficulty matching them with available positions. While they represented a clear minority of all of the temporaries I met, their experiences, which I discuss further below, illustrate the pitfalls and insecurity of temporary employment.

Intermittent Work and Time Off the Job

David Rodriguez, one of the men referred to above, used his time between placements in a perpetual search for a permanent job and additional income. When he was not visiting worksites to submit applications, he worked in the informal economy to earn money. Most of the time he worked for his landlord, cleaning and repairing properties owned by him. As the father of four young children, David desperately wanted to be able to provide for his family. He was industrious in this regard, using whatever skills he could to earn a wage. He was frustrated, though, because he could not find steady, full-time employment.

Terry also worked in the informal economy when she was between placements, providing child care services to relatives, neighbors, and friends. She did not earn a lot of money from child care, but because she lived with her mother and was largely supported by her, she did not feel compelled to take any steady job she could find. She waited patiently for offers of temporary placements, carefully selecting employers and jobs, to gain experience in data entry. As she accumulated that experience, she would apply selectively for regular, full-time employment in the field for which she had trained.

Tom Niles was a fifty-nine-year-old divorced man with three grown children. He had applied for temporary employment almost two months before I met him. It had been ten days since his last placement, one that lasted just six hours. Tom knew, when he accepted that placement, that it was for just one day. "Work is work," he told me. Previously he had three placements of two or three days each.

Apparently because of his age and chronic back pain that made it difficult to work on his feet, Tom had not been able to find a job. He had worked full-time as a mechanic for most of his adult life. When his back pain interfered with his ability to stand and do his job, his employer transferred him to a clerical job. Tom was satisfied with that job and carried out his responsibilities conscientiously. He was fired eight months before I met him, though, unjustifiably Tom believed, and replaced by a young woman who was paid substantially less than what Tom had been paid. Tom had filed an age discrimination suit against his former employer, a suit that was pending when we spoke.

Tom was desperate for a job when he applied for temporary employment. He hoped to find a full-time job through his temporary placements, but that had not happened yet. He was willing to work anytime—day or night—and do almost anything within his physical capabilities. One might think that he would have had steady placements, given his attitude, but instead his placements had been few and of short duration.

Tom was effectively unemployed, but he was without the protections that the work sharers I spoke with had. He was not receiving unemployment insurance benefits, and he had no job to return to. He had applied for state-provided disability benefits. Assuming he was eligible, his financial situation would improve somewhat once he began receiving payments. But he still wanted a job.

How did Tom fill the extra time on his hands? He worked in his yard, tending his flower and vegetable gardens, fruit trees, grapevines, and berry bushes. He canned and froze his produce. His household work was creative and fulfilling because he had time to pursue it leisurely and diligently. It shaded into the realm of recreation. But Tom's financial insecurity limited his full enjoyment of his household work. He worried a lot about money.

Approached from another perspective, Tom's household work was a necessity and, therefore, not especially recreational. He could not afford to purchase a lot of market goods, so he used his time to grow and process some of his own food. He had food to eat despite the fact that he had little income with which to purchase food. Tom's situation harkens back to the image of self-sufficiency associated with the family farm and the romanticized image of the housewife. But he suffered, like her, from the pitfalls of social isolation associated with privatized household work.

As the experiences of these intermittently employed temporaries illustrate, a temporary may be hired for one assignment of one week's duration or less and may not have another assignment for a few days or a few weeks. The next assignment may last a few hours, a few days, a few weeks, or a few months. Because steady employment is not guaranteed, and employment is unpredictable, piecing together a living can be difficult for temporary employees. The irregularity of employment combines in complex ways with financial insecurity to inhibit temporary workers' control of their time and may also contribute to their social isolation.

Ann Price was employed as a temporary for about four months before she took a steady, part-time job. Her part-time job had become a permanent, full-time job shortly before I interviewed her, but her name remained in the THS company's active file. It was the insecurity of temporary employment and the attendant lack of control of time that led Ann to seek other employment.

When Ann signed with the THS company of her choice, she requested full-time positions. She waited about ten days after applying before she received her first placement. That assignment lasted one week, but others followed quickly. Ann worked steadily as a temporary, as she describes below:

> One week they would send you one place, the next week they would send you another place, and then they would send me on a half-week assignment, where I would work Monday through Wednesday, eight to five on Monday and Tuesday and then maybe eight to noon on Wednesday. I would get home Wednesday afternoon and they would call me again and ask, 'Can you be someplace at one and work today and tomorrow?' That's how steady it was. They would call pretty much as soon as I would get done with another assignment.

Ann's experience of temporary employment draws a sharp contrast with those of the intermittently employed temporaries I just described. Although Ann worked steadily as a temporary, she could never be certain when she would have placements or how long they would last. The possibility of unsteady employment and financial insecurity caused Ann great anxiety. She found working temporary jobs "frustrating because you don't know where you're going to be and how long you're going to be there." She coped with her fears that she would have no work by staying home, near the phone, to be sure to be available when the THS company called with a placement for her. If she had worked steadily for several weeks and felt satisfied with her personal finances, Ann occasionally took a long weekend to go out of town and risked missing a phone call on Monday, the phone call that might have offered her a job for the week. She explained the relationship between her personal finances, job insecurity, and her use of time off the job:

It depended on how my financial situation was. If I thought I would be fine for the next month, then I wouldn't worry about it. I'd take a long weekend or whatever. But right when I graduated I needed a lot of money to move out and get a place to live, down payments, and everything, so I really had to push for money. That's exactly what it felt like. I had to be home. I'd probably be home cleaning or doing something anyway, but I felt kind of bad if I wasn't there to get a phone call from the temporary employment company because I would miss out. It was kind of stressful having to worry about whether you'd be working next week or not, even though I did.

Ann's comment that she had to be home reveals the social isolation engendered by temporary employment when it is combined with financial insecurity. Her remarks that she would probably be home anyway illustrate the way in which time off the job is adapted to employment insecurity. The insecurity of employment and unpredictability of her work schedule made Ann feel that her life was "a roller coaster," which she was only able to exit when she found her steady, part-time job with a regular schedule.

Summary and Conclusion

Temporary employment grew at a rapid pace during the 1980s. Whereas this type of employment used to be concentrated among clerical workers, today temporary employment is also found in manual labor, professional, and technical jobs. Employers hire temporaries for reasons similar to part-time workers; they permit employers to reduce labor costs and maximize flexible staffing.

Individuals who work as temporaries do so either because they want to or they cannot find full-time employment. Among voluntary temporaries, variety of worksites and responsibilities, limited control over the work schedule, use of temporary employment as a transitional activity, and opportunity to gain work experience are among the reasons often cited for choosing temporary employment. Involuntary temporaries choose temporary employment as a last resort; they prefer regular, full-time work but cannot find a suitable job. Some involuntary temporaries hope one of their temporary placements will be offered to them permanently, thus they use temporary help supply companies as if they are employment services. One point of contrast with part-time employment clearly stands out: few individuals work as temporaries to integrate wage work and child care. The unpredictability of temporary work, it appears, interferes with responsiveness to children's needs.

My concern in this chapter was with the experience of temporary employment, in particular, how it affects personal autonomy and the quality of life. The regularity of employment, along with the number of hours of employment each week, the nature of the work schedule, and the level of pay influenced individuals' use of time off the job. Most temporaries I met had regular work schedules. Many were employed forty hours a week for several consecutive weeks. They wanted to work as much as possible to earn as much as possible, anticipating that their placements were finite. These individuals complained of the tyranny of the forty-hour week. They had limited free time, because they worked full-time, and they had little discretionary income because their wages were low and insecure. Those with alternative sources of financial support, particularly a husband's income, were able to maximize the flexibility and autonomy often reported to accompany temporary employment.

Individuals with intermittent temporary placements experienced long periods of unemployment. Placements were unpredictable and unsteady. Consequently, they had very much free time but little discretionary income. They used their time off the job working in the informal economy to earn more money and/or in a continuing search for a regular, full-time job. Some complained of social isolation associated with waiting for the THS company to call them with an offer of employment.

In conclusion, the experience of temporary employment depends upon a complex of factors having to do with the frequency and continuity of placements, the nature of the work schedule, the level of pay, and temporary workers' marital status and living arrangements. Some individuals are able to turn insecure employment to their advantage, maximizing flexibility and autonomy. Others experience insecurity as just that, insecurity, and find temporary employment a frustrating substitute for steady, full-time work.

Chapter Six

The Job Sharers

Job sharing differs from conventional part-time employment in two important ways. First, the purpose of job sharing is to restructure career-oriented positions which cannot be reduced in hours or split between two part-time employees. It is at least in theory an effort to reduce individual workers' hours without marginalizing the worker. As I will discuss below, however, job sharing is not always successful in this regard. Second, job sharing often requires a significant degree of cooperation and communication between the partners in a job-sharing arrangement because they must keep each other apprised of their respective accomplishments since they share responsibility for the same job. They also must keep each other informed of matters that arise when one or the other is absent from the office.[1]

In contrast to part-time and temporary employment, market forms of reduced work which have grown as a result of management-led initiatives to reduce labor costs and better respond to market conditions, job sharing often occurs when individuals negotiate with their employers for reduced hours. Job sharing may be a temporary arrangement, but it is also a form of permanent part-time employment. It is usually defined as "two people sharing the responsibility of one full-time position, with salary and fringe benefits prorated."[2] It is designed to increase not only the number of part-time jobs but also the quality of those jobs by prorating salary and fringe benefits. Job sharing is usually voluntary, requested by workers and negotiated with their employers. The practice occurs most often among clerical workers, although it is not uncommon among professionals. Some job sharers work in close partnership; others work more or less independently. In some instances, like academic settings, job sharers are marital partners; in others, job sharers are unrelated but they work in close partnership; and in still others, they never meet but communicate by phone or note.[3]

Job sharers are a miniscule portion of all employed persons in the United States.[4] A survey of job sharers conducted in the late 1970s suggests that the overwhelming majority of job sharers are women, many of whom use job sharing to integrate paid employment with child care. Seventy-seven percent of the 238 respondents to that survey were members of job-sharing teams comprised of two women. Only four percent were members of teams comprised of two men. The remaining 19 percent were members of male/female teams.[5] My research for this book also substantiates the claim that the majority of job sharers are women. Of 400 job sharers who were employed in state government in Michigan in 1986, 355 were women and 55 were men.

In his 1984 State of the State message, Michigan Governor James Blanchard directed all state departments to develop plans to increase shared job arrangements to expand employment options and generate employment opportunities in state government for persons who cannot work on a full-time schedule. Job sharing in Michigan state government may be initiated by employees or managers, is limited to positions that are identical in civil service class and level or those that are similar in nature, and can be arranged only between positions that are in the same department and share common agency number codes, time keeping units, payroll/personnel systems, and county/city location codes. Employees sharing a job may be assigned individual caseloads, individual portions of a job, or may literally share the same job at different scheduled times. Thus, job sharing in Michigan state government takes the form of "job splitting" or "classic" job sharing, the latter involving extensive coordination of job tasks and responsibilities between job-share partners.

The work schedules of Michigan government job sharers vary, reflecting their personal preferences, the requirements of their job, and the State of Michigan's use of flexitime, but the total number of hours worked by all employees involved in a particular shared-job situation cannot exceed eighty hours in a two-week pay period. Employees sharing a job earn annual and sick leave each time they complete eighty hours in pay status. These and other benefits are subject to policy for other part-time employees.

Job sharing in Michigan state government is also subject to existing civil service procedures or collective bargaining provisions as they apply to part-time employment. However, the concept of job sharing and job sharers' rights and obligations are not well defined in current employment guidelines. Because of this uncertainty, job sharers may be vulnerable in areas not governed by civil service regulations or protected by collectively bargained contracts. For example, these documents do not define, other than in the broad terms outlined above, who may job share and under what conditions, therefore supervisors have considerable discretion in approving workers' requests to job share. There is some evidence that job-share arrangements may be approved discriminately to reward highly valued employees. Supervisors also have the power to terminate job-share arrangements. This power creates feelings of insecurity among job sharers who act to prove the arrangement works in order to prevent a supervisor from terminating it. There appears to be no well-defined recourse for workers who believe their job-sharing arrangement has been terminated unfairly, although as union members they can probably follow the conventional grievance procedure.[6]

In 1986 there were 178.5 positions shared by two or more employees in Michigan state government, representing 0.3 percent of all state government positions. Almost 50 percent of job sharers were clerical workers, one-fourth were professionals, and another 20 percent were paraprofessionals. The largest proportion (37.5 percent) of job-share positions were in the Department of Social Services. Nineteen percent were in the Department of Mental Health. Another 29 percent were distributed across the departments of the Attorney General, Education, Natural Resources, and Transportation. Nine other departments accounted for 14 percent of all job-share positions, and eight state departments had no job-share positions.

The job sharers I met were clerical workers, accountants, and caseworkers who had shared jobs, on average, for two years, from six months to seven and one-half years. To the extent that they were defined at all, the procedures they followed to request job sharing, like the terms and conditions of their employment as job sharers, were defined to a large extent by the civil service regulations and labor union contracts that govern state employment. Their reasons for job sharing, however, were quite personal, although there are important similarities among the small group of job sharers I met.

Becoming a Job Sharer

As noted above, most job sharers are women. Most of the job sharers I talked to wanted to share a job because they had young children to care for at home. They were married women, and with the exception of one whose husband was laid off at the time she began to job share (he was reemployed when I interviewed her, however), there was a second earner in the home. All of these women had been employed full-time in state government—some for as long as ten to fifteen years—before they began job sharing. While a few would have continued to work full-time had they not begun to share their job, most would have quit their job under the demands of caring for young children at home.

One woman I spoke with, however, had chosen to share her job for a different reason. She had a second job playing in a band for weddings and at local clubs. Because her performances were customarily on Thursday, Friday, and Saturday nights, job sharing permitted her to work at her day job early in the week, reserving energy for her late-night engagements at the end of the week.

The men I spoke with had other reasons for job sharing. One caseworker had been employed full-time in state government for five years. He was also actively involved in a lay ministry. To increase the amount of time he gave to his religious work, he reduced the hours he devoted to his government job. When we spoke, he was considering quitting his job to pursue his lay ministry full-time. In this instance, job sharing was potentially a mode of exit, an easing out, from employment in state government.

In another case, job sharing was a mode of entry to state employment. One man had been a self-employed accountant for many years. He had grown tired of the constant pressure to keep his business going, and he was particularly unhappy with his lack of free time. He applied for a full-time job in state government; what became available initially was half of a job-share position. He accepted that position to break into the civil service system and hoped that eventually he would move into a full-time slot.

The latter case suggests that people who share jobs do not always do so as a first preference and do not always actively seek to do so. In my interviews with job sharers, I discovered several paths to job sharing: workers initially requested part-time hours; workers were courted by coworkers who wanted to share a job; or workers were offered advertised half-positions. Only one case fit the standard interpretation of job sharing, that a worker negotiates with an employer to share his or her job and locates a suitable job-share partner. Most of the people I spoke with had actually requested part-time employment when they approached their supervisors initially or when they had their names added to a "part-time list" in the Department of Civil Service. Their requests took this form because they were not familiar with the practice of job sharing or aware that it was an employment option, not because they did not want to job share. They were more familiar with the notion of conventional part-time employment, and their main concern was with reducing their hours from full-time status to part-time. They were less concerned with the actual form of their part-time employment. In most cases, these individuals were eventually informed of job-share options in their office or another office (in the latter instance, they had to apply to transfer) and introduced to coworkers who were interested in job sharing. Once such introductions were made, the partners entered into a negotiation process to determine their work schedules, how they would divide their responsibilities, and the like. In one case, however, half of a job-share position had been advertised when one partner vacated the slot. In this case, the replacement inherited the previously determined responsibilities and work schedule. In another instance, a full-time accountant's position was converted to job-share status, and the newly created half-position was advertised.

Negotiating a job-share arrangement can become a courtship of sorts. A couple of women I met had had no interest in job sharing initially. When they were first approached by coworkers who wanted to share their job, they flat out said no. Their coworkers were relentless, however, and they eventually persuaded these women to try job sharing. One of the initially resistant women had actually shared a job for more than seven years when I met her. Her experience had made her a convert. She had become a champion of job sharing and had no intention of returning to a full-time work schedule so long as she and her husband could afford it.

Sometimes the job-share arrangement was established by supervisors. In these instances, workers approached management with a request for part-time hours. In an effort to grant that request, supervisors created job-share positions, particularly if they were aware of another worker in the office who also wanted part-time hours. They might also convert the requesting worker's full-time position to job-share status and then advertise the newly created half-time slot. For one woman I spoke with, however, becoming a job sharer in this way meant accepting two demotions. She had been employed full-time as a secretary to her department's personnel director. Because her supervisors were not willing to let her share that job, she had to take a position as a receptionist in which she had fewer, and more routine, responsibilities and for which she received less pay. Another woman, whose full-time position was converted to job-share status with the new half-position subsequently posted, was excluded from the process to hire her job-share partner despite her requests to participate. Her appeals, regarding the importance of compatibility when coworkers must communicate well to coordinate their job responsibilities, were unconvincing to her supervisors.

As these cases illustrate, how individuals become job sharers varies somewhat, but in all instances they must obtain supervisory approval to share a job and supervisors must approve job sharers' work schedules if workers negotiate their own schedules. Supervisors exercise considerable discretionary power because they must approve all job-share arrangements and partners' work schedules, and because formal policy governing job sharing in Michigan state government is incomplete. Despite the governor's directive to expand part-time options, supervisors' power to resist job sharing is strong, as one woman I spoke with indicated when she said that the personnel director in her unit "had to be fought all the way" despite her immediate supervisor's approval of her job-sharing plan. Many supervisors do not like job sharing because it increases their work. For example, a supervisor who ordinarily manages ten full-time employees would oversee twenty if all of those positions were converted to job-share status. Thus, job sharing requires additional personnel management and recordkeeping, and sometimes extra training sessions or other meetings must be scheduled to accommodate absent job sharers. Attitudes toward individual workers may influence supervisors to approve or reject requests for job sharing, as one accountant told me. She believed that job sharing is a reward given discriminately to valued employees. Supervisors may terminate job-share arrangements that they think are not working, creating a heightened sense of insecurity among job sharers who very much want to continue the arrangement, and supervisory turnover may alter the conditions under which partners job share. One woman felt that she and her partner were given "the crud jobs" when a new supervisor reorganized task divisions in their office. The jobs of similarly classified full-time clerks were upgraded, giving those workers higher pay and more opportunities to advance, but the job-share position was not upgraded. The new supervisor had also questioned the pair's career commitment. The job sharers interpreted these acts as affronts directed at part-time employees by a supervisor prejudiced against part-time workers. Their experience contradicts an argument often made in favor of job sharing, that is, that it upgrades jobs.[7] In this case, the job was degraded (or at least not upgraded when other jobs in the office were upgraded), and the partners were stigmatized much like conventional part-time workers.

In sum, people who job share do so for various reasons. Most job sharers are women seeking to integrate paid employment and child care responsibilities. Some people choose to job share to balance other non-job-related activities with employment, such as education, alternative employment, and community activities. Job sharing may also be a first step toward full-time employment in an organization that is difficult to break into or the first step toward leaving a job for another, more preferable pursuit. The means by which workers become job sharers also vary depending upon the particular circumstances within the office where they are employed and how supervisors exercise their discretion in granting the job-share option.

Job Sharers' Work Schedules

Generally, job sharers who work for the State of Michigan work forty hours in a two-week pay period and negotiate their own schedules. Their schedules are subject to supervisory approval, although sometimes supervisors create the task division between job sharers as well as their work schedules. Sometimes the work schedule is inherited from the partner being replaced.

Job sharers' work schedules vary, reflecting the individual needs and preferences of workers and the demands of the office where they are employed. Most of the job sharers I talked to worked the same two days each week and rotated a third. For example, one partner might work Tuesday and Thursday each week, the other partner then works Monday and Friday each week, and they rotate Wednesdays. Or one partner might work Monday and Wednesday each week, the other partner works Tuesday and Thursday each week, and they rotate Fridays. Others alternated weeks, either Monday through Friday or midweek to midweek. One woman who worked Wednesday through Tuesday in an alternating weekly arrangement noted that she and her partner "always have a weekend to break up the week." The workweek was then followed by an entire week off.

Because the State of Michigan uses flexitime, daily work schedules also varied among the job sharers I met. Some of them worked from 8:00 AM to 5:00 PM with an hour for lunch. Others worked from 8:30 AM to 5:00 PM or 7:30 AM to 4:00 PM or 7:00 AM to 3:30 PM with a half hour for lunch. Several preferred working full days instead of half days to maximize effort on the job and economize on time associated with commuting, dressing for work, and taking children to a day-care center. One partnership would have forgone job sharing entirely if they had had to work half days.

Several of the job sharers I interviewed had experimented with different schedules before settling on one. One partnership, for example, tried an alternating weekly schedule until that proved to be confusing to coworkers, so they shifted to the same two or three days each week to "keep things more structured at work and at home."

The ability to control and alter the work schedule in response to personal preferences, changes in day-care arrangements, the office environment, and other constraints contributes to making job sharing a distinctive form of part-time employment. Among all of the persons I interviewed who work less than full-time, the ability to control the work schedule appears to be related to the type of reduced work. Of the women and men I met who controlled their work schedules, eight were in job-share arrangements, four were employed in more conventional part-time jobs, and three were temporaries. The eight job sharers were about three-fourths of all of the job sharers I interviewed; the four part-time workers were almost half of all of the part-time workers I interviewed; and the three temporaries were one-fourth of all of the temporaries I interviewed. Thus it appears that job sharers are most likely to have considerable control over their work schedules, part-time workers may or may not have such control, and temporaries are least likely to be able to determine their work schedules beyond stating broad preferences on their temporary employment application form.

Most of the people I spoke with who controlled their work schedules were employed in the public sector. This is largely a function of the fact that most of the job sharers I met were state government employees. But job sharers in the private sector have a large degree of control over their work schedule, too. It is the nature of job sharing to enhance worker autonomy over conditions of employment such as the scheduling of work to accommodate non-job-related obligations and responsibilities.

With one exception, all of the individuals I spoke with who controlled their work schedule were women. The intersection of reduced work and the sex/gender system accounts for this phenomenon. Most of the persons employed in job-sharing arrangements or in more conventional part-time jobs—the forms of reduced work where the ability to control one's work schedule seems to be concentrated—are women, and many of them are mothers. Attempts to control the work schedule are especially urgent among women juggling the responsibilities of wage work and child care.

For persons with a large degree of control over their work schedule, the work schedule represents a multifaceted compromise among their child care concerns (or some other non-job-related activity), their desire for employment, the similar concerns and desires of the job-share partner (among those who job share), and the requirements of their employer. Several factors influence the selection of optimum work schedules by employed mothers: smooth coordination of employment and substitute child care arrangements, husband's work schedule, minimizing confusion among coworkers that might develop when one's work schedule is unconventional, commuting, and personal circadian rhythms and work habits. One of the advantages of workers' control of the work schedule is the opportunity to experiment with different schedules to determine one that is most suitable. Another advantage is that work schedules can be rearranged to better accommodate changes in personal circumstances. Such flexibility in the work schedule also permits workers to make changes in their personal lives, perhaps by integrating new activities, because they know they can adjust their work schedules to accommodate the new activities. In this way, the work schedule is no longer a hindrance to taking on new and varied activities since it can be altered to accommodate them.

Job Sharing and Time Off the Job

The job sharers I met repeatedly told me that they had "the best of both worlds." As a group, they perceived a richness and balance in their lives unmatched by most of the other people I interviewed. Job sharing enhanced employed mothers' relationships with their children, relieved stress by giving women more time to manage their household responsibilities, and freed up time for recreational activities and community service among women and men. Self-esteem among the women who shared their job was high because they had families they loved and jobs that gave them an identity other than the too often maligned "wife and mother." Some recent research has suggested that paid employment has become increasingly central in many women's lives. Multiple work and family roles may be stressful, leading to role strain, role conflict, and role overload, or they may enhance one another and individual well-being. The positive or negative consequences of multiple roles may be a function of the degree of flexibility in structural arrangements.[8] Indeed, among the job-sharing women I met, the flexibility and autonomy gained by sharing a job and the ability to control one's work schedule seemed to contribute to a heightened sense of individual well-being.

Balancing Employment and Child Care

Many women who are employed full-time seek to work part-time when they enter the childbearing phase of their lives. This adjustment in work time may be seen as an effort to integrate a new activity, childrearing, into their lives. As noted above, the majority of job sharers I met were employed mothers who chose to reduce their work hours to balance employment and child care. Consequently, much of their time off the job was devoted to child care. As wage-earning women, they liked having a job outside the home, and, in most instances, their income was a necessary addition to that of their husband. As mothers, however, they believed it important to be involved in their children's lives by spending time at home with them, being available to take them to various activities, and participating in school-related programs. They found time for such involvement by reducing their hours of employment.

Relieving the Double Burden

Many of the job-sharing women I met said spending less time on the job relieved stress at home. Their work schedules permitted them to shift household work from evenings and weekends to other times during the week, freeing evenings and weekends for other activities. They did their household work at a slower, more enjoyable pace with more satisfactory results. Elaine Bowman, for example, told me she spent most of her time off job doing what she would "otherwise do," but she did not feel rushed doing it. For Elaine, working less than full-time meant her house was cleaner and she could do household work more slowly and spread it over several days. Her experience provides some insight into the relationship between household work and autonomy. Most everyone I spoke with perceived household work as work that had to be done, although some tasks may be more or less enjoyable. In this sense, there is little autonomy in household work because it must be done. The autonomy comes, however, in the household worker's ability to decide what to do (to select from an array of tasks that must be done—although even this can be influenced by the needs of other household members and cultural conventions) and when to do it. By working less than full-time, people do not have to try to complete household work in a small, perhaps fixed amount of time, for example, weekends. Barbara Worrell's remarks are instructive in this regard. She told me that when she worked full-time she did "absolutely everything" on weekends, and what she could not accomplish on weekends overflowed into her evenings during the week. She resented working full-time because she felt that she had little choice over when to do household work. She felt forced to do grocery shopping and laundry, for example, at night because there were not enough hours on the weekend to complete all of her household tasks.

Such is the tyranny of the forty-hour workweek. Full-time workers spend their evenings and weekends racing against the clock, taking care of household responsibilities and other obligations, perhaps finding time to watch a movie or have a family picnic before the workweek begins again on Monday. The breakneck speed at which they must go, in order to do everything they want to do, takes its toll in the form of individual stress and household tension. They live life constantly feeling that they are running behind, trying to catch up, but never quite making it. Eventually something's got to give.

Kathy Teasley's stress was immediately visible to anyone who took the time to notice. Her drooped shoulders, rapid-fire speech punctuated with heavy sighs, and darting, intense brown eyes told me she was under a great deal of pressure long before she made that verbal proclamation. She had been job sharing for three years, which relieved some of her stress, but she still shouldered a heavy weight of responsibility at home.

A clerical worker, Kathy worked full-time for ten years until her first child, her son, was six months old. He was a "terrible sleeper" with whom Kathy wrestled nightly to try to put him down to sleep. Once she got him down, her victory was temporary as he would never sleep through the night. Night after night of interrupted sleep wore Kathy down. If she had not been able to find a part-time position, she would have quit her job despite the fact that her husband was unemployed at the time. As Kathy explained to me,

> When you work full-time, and even when you have children, you think you should be able to keep up with everything. And it bothers me a lot when I can't. I get ornery, and I take it out on my husband. I have a short temper with the kids.

Kathy's son was four years old when we spoke, and she had a six-month-old infant daughter. Her son had outgrown the difficulties that led Kathy to seek part-time work, but now she had two children to care for. Kathy's husband, a construction worker, did not share child care or household work with her. When he was home, he tinkered in the garage and left the "woman's work" to Kathy.

Job sharing permits many women to spend more time with their children and relieves some of the stress associated with employment, child care, and household responsibilities. The benefits of job sharing for women in many instances, however, are subsidized by the financial support of their husbands. In this way, job sharing in particular, and reduced work more generally, does not challenge conventional gender relations. Instead, it reinforces them. Reducing hours of employment is an accommodation women make to the excessive demands of employment, child care, household responsibilities, and other commitments. It relieves some of the stress associated with their "double burden," but it does not remove the responsibilities associated with multiple spheres of activity, nor does it necessarily equalize the distribution of these varied responsibilities across women and their husbands.

Time Left Over for Recreation

After child care and household work, recreational activities were the off-the-job activities mentioned most frequently by the men and women I spoke with who were in job-share arrangements. For some, these activities included other family members or friends. For others, recreation was an opportunity for solitude. But for others, the demands of child care, household work, and other activities left little free time for recreation despite the reduction in their hours of employment.

Recreation included a broad array of activities pursued by the women and men I met: individual and team sports; outdoor activities such as gardening, camping, hunting, fishing, and boating; indoor activities such as sewing, crafts, knitting, reading, and computers; spectator activities such as sports, movies, and television viewing; and artistic pursuits such as music, painting, dance, and photography. What these varied activities have in common is that they are pursued for their own sake (they are ends in themselves even though they produce a product in some cases); they are pleasurable for the individual who does them; and they are sources of escape, relaxation, or rejuvenation.

Yet recreation and household work or child care are difficult to separate, particularly for women. A family camping trip, for example, involves food preparation, clean up, and supervision of children— tasks that are typically women's responsibility. Sewing often produces clothing for oneself and other household members and may be an activity selected as a less expensive alternative to ready-to-wear clothing. Garden produce must be picked, it is often cooked before it is consumed, and large yields may be canned or frozen for future use. Women's leisure scholar Rosemary Deem notes that housework and leisure frequently overlap in women's daily lives. This occurs because women often pursue recreational activities that can be performed easily in and around the house in the presence of others and, like some household tasks, are readily adaptable to small quantities of time.[9] The women and men I spoke with, however, made it clear that they had separate conceptions of household work and recreation. Many implied that some activities must be done whether they are enjoyable or not. This attitude colored their discussions of what I categorize as household work. The pleasurability, or lack thereof, however, is not necessarily an inherent quality of the task. An ordinarily unpleasant task could become enjoyable if one was not rushed in accomplishing it, if one had some choice over when to do it, or if it could be done in the company of others. Recreational activities, by contrast, are unequivocally pleasurable, at least among the women and men I met, when they are a matter of personal choice.

As noted above, job sharing freed time for recreational pursuits for many of the people I spoke with. Some women, however, had difficulty finding time for recreation despite the reduction in time devoted to their jobs and the ability to control their work schedule. Among the job sharers, Kathy Teasley is the best example of a woman with little free time. Because her husband offered little help in caring for their children or their home, Kathy had little relief from these responsibilities. When we spoke, however, Kathy had recently rebelled against her husband's lock on personal leisure time and had found a little time for herself. Kathy had begun attending a jazzercise class for one hour one evening a week, which she described as her "hour out." "Being so tied down to the house and kids was really getting to me this summer," Kathy explained to me, "and I just needed something by myself, to get away. It's not getting away taking the kids to the store." Kathy's husband had offered some resistance when she announced that she wanted to take a jazzercise class. "You go out all the time," he had said. Kathy sneered when she recounted the story to me. "Taking the kids shopping with me is not a release!" she had protested emphatically.

Other women found time for recreational pursuits, but some interests remained unfulfilled. Susan Greenwell bowled in a league once a week which gave her a respite from her household responsibilities and an opportunity to visit with family and friends on her team. Her husband cared for their children on her night out in exchange for Susan's caring for the children on his night out. This ethic of reciprocity governed their relationship, making the Greenwell's relationship one of the more egalitarian I heard about. But Susan still bumped up against limits on her recreational activities, although these limits appeared to be a matter of her own creation.

Susan very much wanted to take a crafts class on her days off, but she was reluctant to do so because she would have to leave her children with a substitute caretaker to do so. Because her children already stayed with a caretaker on the days Susan went to the office, Susan was reluctant to leave them on her days off. As she explained to me,

> I brought these two children into the world, and I can't be gone from them all the time. I'm gone Monday, Wednesday, and every other Friday, and I don't feel that it's right to leave them on Tuesday and Thursday.... I figure a lot of things I want to do are put on hold temporarily, and I guess in the back of my mind I know if I want to do it bad enough, I'll do it later. Right now, that's not the most important thing.

Susan's commentary reveals her ideology of motherhood and emphasizes the responsibility and self-sacrifice associated with parenting. Indeed, parenting is a huge responsibility, and children's needs often must come first. Yet in the gender politics of self-sacrifice, women often sacrifice more than men. They sacrifice education, career, income, recreation, and sometimes sanity. Susan Greenwell's evening out, however, provided her with sufficient free time that she did not exhibit the restlessness and angst that I saw in Kathy Teasley. Nor did Susan Greenwell feel guilty about her evening out, for she believed she deserved it, she earned it, and it was fair that she get it. She accommodated her husband at times, minding the children so he could go bowling or take a class; so he should accommodate her.

Susan and Jerry Greenwell also believed they should each have time alone with their children to foster independent relationships with them. Sometimes one of them would spend time with both children (giving the other parent some free time); sometimes they would divide the children between them. The Greenwells had institutionalized a weekly ritual in which this pairing of parent and child occurred. One Thursday evening Jerry spent time with their son, perhaps taking him out for the evening meal, and Susan spent time with their daughter. The next Thursday evening the parents traded children; Jerry spent time with their daughter, and Susan spent time with their son. By ritualizing these one-on-one parent/child encounters in just this way, each parent was assured of developing an independent relationship with each child.

Given the ethic of reciprocity and ideology of parenting that govern the Greenwell household, Susan should have been able to take that crafts class she wanted to take. But her responsibility to her children prevented her from doing so. If she could have left her children with their father instead of with a caretaker, however, I am certain she would have taken that crafts class without guilt. So the real issue for

Susan was not that she should spend her days off with her children, but that her children should not have to spend more time with a caretaker who is not a parent. If Jerry could have been available during the day, Susan's problem would have been solved. But Jerry was not available because he worked full-time. At one point in our conversation, I asked Susan if she thought her husband would consider working part-time. She reasoned that he might if she had a better paying job, but she was not sure he would do it over the long term. There is the rub. In an economy in which men generally earn more than women, a couple's rational choice is to have the woman forego income by working part-time and the man work full-time to maximize household income. And if a man is a man at all, according to prevailing cultural definitions of masculinity, he will want to work full-time because it is his role to provide for his family. While Susan Greenwell had a balanced life of employment, family, and recreation and a husband who shared child care with her because of the ethic of reciprocity and child rearing practices they had agreed to, she and Jerry Greenwell did not have a perfectly egalitarian relationship. What inequity existed in their relationship came from social structural sources over which they had little control. They had done the best they could in their small, interpersonal sphere to effect as egalitarian a relationship as possible.

Making Time for Community Service

Not all of the job sharers I met engaged in community service, nor did job sharing "cause" community service among those who did. With few exceptions, those who volunteered in their churches, schools, and other organizations did so when they were employed full-time and continued their participation after reducing their work hours. However, like the caseworker discussed above who decided to share a job so he could give more time to his lay ministry, some increased the time they devoted to community service once they began giving less time to their job; others took on new community activities facilitated by the reduction in their hours of employment.

Many of the women I met who shared jobs volunteered as scout troop leaders and room mothers in the schools. Their choice of community activities was an extension of their roles as mothers. Participating in such activities was one way of deepening involvement in their children's lives. Their experiences are consistent with the results of a recent survey on volunteers in the United States. About 20 percent of all Americans provide unpaid work to a wide variety of organizations and institutions. More than half (56 percent) of all volunteers are women.

Volunteers are most likely to be between the ages of thirty-five and forty-four, married with children, and well educated. Indeed, having children seems to open up volunteer opportunities as schools and scouting organizations look to parents for additional labor power.[10]

How did job sharing facilitate community service among those who took on new community activities? Principally by permitting job sharers to reclaim the day. The women who served as room mothers had to be available during school hours to escort children on field trips, to help prepare and manage class picnics, and the like. Quite obviously, someone who works a standard full-time job, from eight to five Monday through Friday, is not available for such activities. Therefore, by freeing some daytime hours, job sharing increased the community service options for those inclined to do volunteer work.

For others, job sharing simply created more free time and, therefore, time that could be devoted to community service. One woman began to fulfill her desire to volunteer only after she began job sharing. Barbara Worrell had worked full-time for fifteen years, raising two children during that time. As much as she would have liked to stay home with those children, she and her husband could not afford her quitting her job. By the time Barbara became pregnant with their third child, in her late thirties, she and her husband were more financially secure. Barbara had planned to quit her job when the third child was born, but the household's financial security proved to be temporary. Barbara's husband's company had failed by the time she gave birth to their third child, about the time that one of Barbara's coworkers had begun asking her to share a job. In an effort to balance her desires to stay home with what she knew would be her last child and her need to attend to her family's weakened financial standing, Barbara agreed to share her coworker's job.

As a result of her decision to spend more time with her new daughter, Barbara gradually became increasingly involved in community service activities. She participated in a day-care cooperative when her daughter was a preschooler, and she became an officer in the home-school organization after her daughter began elementary school. During our conversation, Barbara told me that these types of activities were something she had always wanted to do, but she had never had the time for them before. While these activities were extensions of Barbara's identity as a mother, they also satisfied her as a person. Because they were activities she had always wanted to do, her life was incomplete and she remained somewhat unsatisfied until she had the opportunity to do them.

As this analysis of time off the job reveals, job-sharing women in particular use this time to care for children and do household work. Because they devote fewer hours to their paid job, they can devote more hours to their household responsibilities and they can pursue these dual spheres of activity with less stress. Some job sharers also had more time for recreational pursuits and community service. Women's ability to engage in these types of activities depended to some degree on the gender politics in their household and their ability to get away by themselves.

Summary and Conclusion

Job sharing can be a form of permanent, part-time employment. It differs from conventional part-time employment because salary and benefits are usually prorated, and there is more job security with job sharing than conventional part-time work. Because job sharing is usually voluntary, there are few individuals who share a job who would actually prefer a regular, full-time schedule. Most job sharers negotiate their work schedule with their job-share partner and their supervisor, seeking to maximize their temporal autonomy by establishing a schedule that provides an optimum balance of a myriad of activities. This is perhaps the main attraction of job sharing: the worker's ability to reduce *and* schedule the hours of paid work. In the particular cases I studied, however, supervisors had considerable discretionary power to approve or disapprove job-sharing arrangements and work schedules as well as the authority to terminate job-sharing arrangements that they perceived were problematic. This led job sharers to be ever vigilant to the attitudes of supervisors and coworkers in order to avoid causing problems for them and risk losing the job-share option.

For women in particular, reduced hours of paid work leave more time to share meaningful activities with children, devote to community service, and engage in recreational pursuits. Because these women control their work schedules, they can adjust the timing of employment on a daily or weekly basis to get the "best fit" of employment and other activities and responsibilities. They can adjust their work schedule to accommodate a child's caretaker's schedule, for example, and they can experiment with different schedules in the process of determining the best one. The knowledge that the schedule can be changed if necessary enhances women's sense of control over their lives.

The reduction of hours relieves the stress of the double burden—the responsibilities of paid work and household work. Women can manage housework more autonomously because they have more time available to do it, and they may have time left over which they may use for recreational activities that rejuvenate the body and spirit. The responsibilities associated with child care and the gender politics in a woman's household may limit her temporal autonomy, however, despite the reduction in her hours of employment and her control over her work schedule. She may find herself with little time left over—little time for herself, little time which she may use for recreational purposes for participating in the community—if she is the primary child caretaker because her husband abdicates responsibility in this sphere of activity. In this case, reduced work reinforces traditional gender relations rather than challenging them. Controlling the work schedule in this instance enables women to gain a better sense of control over their employment and household responsibilities, but their structural position remains a subordinate one. They also remain largely isolated in the household when they are not at their job, and their spirit is malnourished under the heavy weight of their household responsibilities.

Chapter Seven

The Work Sharers

Work sharing differs from job sharing in that it is a strategy for rationing the available wage work. Industrial societies have consistently applied policies to reduce and ration working time as a means of decreasing joblessness. Approaches have varied, ranging from temporary and permanent reductions of the workweek to systematically removing various sections of the working-age population from the labor force through, for example, prolonged schooling in youth or early retirement.[1]

Generally, work sharing takes two basic forms. One type seeks to reduce working time among the employed to create jobs for the unemployed, thus distributing available wage work more evenly among a larger number of persons. Legislated reductions of the workweek are one example here. This type has been used with the intent of reducing unemployment caused by long-term structural conditions that are likely to persist beyond the periodic downturns of the business cycle. A second type occurs under conditions of slack work and is usually restricted to specific firms; it is used as a short-term strategy to prevent layoffs and dismissals by temporarily reducing working time. For example, employers and employees in a given firm may decide to temporarily reduce the workweek and earnings by 10 percent as an alternative to laying off one-tenth of existing workers.[2] Advocates of this form of work time reduction note that work sharing is a form of affirmative action. By retaining low seniority workers on the job, work sharing extracts women and minorities, typically workers with low seniority, from the cycle of last hired, first fired.[3]

Work time reductions to decrease unemployment have most commonly occurred in the form of shortened workweeks. In the post-World War II period, approximately 30 percent of collective bargaining agreements have had formal provisions for work sharing, although, with the exception of the highly unstable garment industries, these options have rarely been used. More recently, short workweeks were used as an alternative to layoffs by a number of firms in the New York metropolitan area during the dual crises of the 1975 recession and city fiscal crisis.[4] Since the late 1970s, at least eleven states—California, Arizona, Oregon, Washington, Florida, Maryland, Illinois, Arkansas, Texas, Louisiana, and New York—have instituted short-time compensation programs which permit qualifying employers to cut their workers' hours and the workers in turn can receive prorated unemployment insurance benefits.[5]

In 1979, less than 2 percent of the total number of persons employed were work sharers. While male work sharers outnumbered women by 5 percent and whites far outnumbered racial minorities, women and racial minorities were disproportionately represented, relative to their percentage of the working population. Work sharers were concentrated among blue-collar workers, with the largest proportion of work sharers holding jobs as operatives and craft workers. The incidence of work sharing also varied by industry. The construction, manufacturing, and trade sectors accounted for disproportionate numbers of work sharers.[6]

The work sharers I interviewed during my research for this book had volunteered to be laid off temporarily under an inverse seniority layoff plan in an aging automobile plant in which one of two assembly lines was permanently shut down. Usually workers in automobile companies are laid off in order of seniority from least to highest. Under the inverse plan, high seniority workers in certain job categories volunteered to be laid off for four months, seven months, or one year. Less senior workers stayed on the job and accrued seniority toward transfer rights and supplemental unemployment benefits (SUB).

Work sharers generally suffer a loss of wages associated with the reduction in their hours, although those who are eligible for short-time compensation make up some of that wage loss in prorated unemployment insurance benefits. Because they remain attached to their job, instead of being laid off, work sharers on short-time compensation can retain their fringe benefits.[7] The work sharers I spoke with, however, drew regular unemployment insurance because they were laid off. They maintained health insurance coverage while they were laid off as part of the work sharing deal, but they lost other benefits.

Choosing Unemployment

As noted above, the work sharers I spoke with were employed at an aging automobile plant in Michigan. They had volunteered to be laid off temporarily under an inverse seniority layoff scheme when their employer announced the permanent shutdown of one of two assembly lines. In 1987 General Motors managers announced that one of two production lines at this facility would be permanently shutdown, displacing 3,400 workers. More than one thousand high-seniority workers volunteered to be laid off under the inverse plan. The inverse seniority layoff plan was developed by the company and the union, in tandem with the more commonplace system of indefinite layoffs according to seniority from low to high. Under the inverse plan, high seniority workers were favored for layoff. Without this plan, these workers would have been required to stay on the job while an equivalent number of low-seniority workers would have been laid off, many without supplemental unemployment benefits and transfer rights. For those low-seniority workers, layoff might have amounted to permanent job loss. Under the inverse layoff scheme, however, low-seniority workers stayed on the job accruing credit for service that could give them supplemental unemployment benefits and transfer rights at some point in the future.

Workers volunteered for the inverse layoff by completing forms provided by local union representatives. They could take the layoff for four months (June layoff with October callback), seven months (June layoff with January callback), or one year (June layoff with May callback). They indicated their preferences on the form with no guarantee that they would be selected to be laid off or that they would get their first choice for period of layoff. Layoffs were contingent upon job classification and seniority. Workers in some job classifications were not eligible at all for the inverse layoff; others had insufficient seniority (generally, less than about fourteen years) despite being in an eligible job classification.

I spoke with a small group of work sharers whose combined seniority was 243 years. Individually their seniority ranged from fourteen to thirty years. The group's average seniority was 20.25 years. When they were laid off, the majority worked as machine operators (e.g. forklift and sweeper drivers) and as laborers (e.g. assemblers, inspectors, metal finishers, and trim finishers). Most had volunteered to be laid off for seven months or one year. Just one took the layoff for four months. Financial considerations were the primary factor in work sharers' decisions to select a layoff period of a particular length. When

I interviewed them, they had been laid off for almost four months. Thus, most had several months left before they would be called back to the plant.

The UAW is widely recognized as a trendsetter in benefits for workers. Under the inverse seniority plan, workers lost some employer-provided benefits, particularly dental and vision insurance and educational tuition assistance. They maintained health insurance coverage, however. Paid sick leave, holidays, and vacations, of course, did not pertain under the layoff. But with state unemployment insurance and SUB, they continued to receive 90 to 95 percent of straight-time pay while laid off. Therefore, despite their not working, the work sharers had incomes for the period of time they were laid off. They also had the security of knowing that they had a job to which they could return at the end of the layoff period and they could request an early return if they preferred, unlike workers laid off under conventional layoff schemes. The work sharers I met, however, did express some doubt about whether they would return to the same job classification or the same work schedule. The 1987 contract negotiations were to take place while they were laid off, and they had heard that some job classifications might be eliminated under the new local agreement. Some had also heard that schedule changes might be made. They were unsure as to what these changes would mean for them personally.

Would not everyone volunteer to receive an income without having to work for it, if given the chance? While I did not speak to workers eligible for the inverse layoff who did not volunteer to be laid off, it is clear that those who did volunteer had weighed the pros and cons and given the matter considerable thought, although they had just a few days to complete and return their preference forms. For example, there were important financial matters to consider. While they were protected from huge income losses if they volunteered to be laid off, they would lose 5 to 10 percent of their straight-time pay and opportunities to work overtime and gain accompanying premium pay. For some, overtime pay is a significant sum of money. Those with home and vehicle loans would have to continue to make payments while laid off. And with the loss of dental and vision insurance coverage, workers would have to cover those costs for themselves and their family.

So just why did they volunteer to be laid off? Among the work sharers I met, there was no single reason but a variety of reasons that motivated them to take the inverse layoff. Many said it was an opportunity to take an extended period of time off, an opportunity that they had never had before and that they anticipated never having again. Many had altruistic motives, wanting to give coworkers with less seniority an opportunity to stay on the job, accruing seniority toward SUB and transfer rights. Those who were near retirement thought an extended layoff would enable them to see how it feels to be off a long time without committing themselves to retirement yet. Others wanted to use their time while laid off to explore alternative employment options, avoid an anticipated contract-year strike (which did not happen), or repair damaged family relationships.

Only one man I spoke with mentioned specifically job-related stress as a factor in his decision to volunteer to be laid off, but the nature of work in automobile plants must be taken into consideration to fully understand why autoworkers might look enthusiastically upon the prospect of extended time off the job. Automobile production work is extremely repetitive and routine. It is the epitome of what sociologists call alienating labor in industrialized societies. Workers on the assembly line stay at their work station with a few short breaks and a break for lunch. They repeat the same motions over and over again, hour after hour, day after day, in synch with the line's movement, becoming a robot-like extension of the machines that make up the assembly line itself. Workers have little job autonomy. They have little decision making power over how their job is performed or the pace at which they must work.[8] The work may be physically demanding, requiring workers to bend and reach or make other contorted movements in a few seconds' time. Like cashiers at the supermarket and others whose work requires them to make the same movements over and over again, automobile workers may develop carpal tunnel syndrome or other painful conditions produced by unnatural repetitive motions. And automobile plants are noisy. There is the constant hum of the assembly line and fans (the old plants are not air conditioned) periodically interrupted by a blast from a rivet gun or a flash from a welding torch (today, often operated by mechanical robots). Work stations are usually sufficiently far apart that conversation between coworkers is difficult if not impossible over the constant drone of background noise. (In newer plants, where teamwork is becoming the norm, there is greater opportunity for social interaction among workers). The plant has a prison-like quality, bounded by factory gates and closed to all but authorized personnel. Workers' vernacular clearly demarcates life "in there" and "on the outside," making the distinction between regimentation and freedom. For high-seniority workers, the layoff was a chance to "get out," a kind of extended prison furlough.

Another aspect of the riddle of work sharing is the declining competitive position of the U.S. automobile industry. The men and women I spoke with worked in an old, two-story plant, a less efficient design than the sprawling, one-story facilities built today. One man told me that he thought his plant had no production schedule after 1990, suggesting to him that the entire operation might be shut down at that time. (As yet there has been no official announcement that the plant will close.) The uncertainty in the domestic auto industry means insecurity and vulnerability for autoworkers, particularly middle-aged workers who would not have retirement as an option should their plant close.

Conditions in the automobile industry today are, of course, quite different from the era when these high-seniority workers first sought employment in automobile plants. Workers near retirement age entered the plants almost thirty years ago and found relatively secure, well-paying jobs for unskilled laborers. Indeed, many of these workers had not completed high school. Those who first became automobile workers fifteen to twenty years ago were more likely to be high school graduates. They worked a lot of overtime and made lots of money, and the money became its own seduction. For some, fifteen to twenty years' seniority is so sufficient an investment of time that they do not want to be forced to make a career change. For others, particularly those who had not intended to stay in the plants that long, insecurity in the domestic automobile industry is the stick encouraging them to finally make a career change that they had intended to make some time ago.

In sum, the work sharers that I spoke to volunteered to be laid off temporarily for a myriad of reasons. The inverse layoff was an opportunity for relatively secure, high-seniority workers to have extended time off the job, an opportunity they rarely obtained. Individuals near retirement used the inverse layoff to "try" retirement before they had to commit themselves to it. Others used their time, while laid off, to explore alternative employment options, participate in the community, and/or repair damaged interpersonal relationships.

Work Schedules Left Behind

Automobile workers have rigid work schedules, although some workers in some job classifications may start working before their official starting time to have more control over their work and to take advantage of optimum working conditions in the plant. One fork-truck driver, for example, told me he started work at 2:30 PM (when first shift goes home and an hour before second shift starts), so he could transport loads in his area while there were few workers on the floor. In his time in the plant, he had observed such careless antics as workers dashing under his load or between his truck and a wall as he was backing up to the wall. He feared for his coworkers' safety and chose to start work early, when there were few other workers in the plant so he could reduce some of his own anxiety on the job. Most of the autoworkers I met, however, had little control over their work schedules and could not alter their schedules, for whatever reasons. Their plant was organized into two shifts, and starting and quitting times varied somewhat by job classification. Generally, first shift began at 6:00 AM, when the line started, and ended at 2:30 PM. Second shift started at 3:30 PM and ended at midnight. Autoworkers who do not work on the line and who do work in preparation for the line start to work earlier than the line does, for example at 5:30 AM or 2:30 PM. Most of the autoworkers with whom I spoke ordinarily worked first shift. Some ordinarily worked second shift, and one man worked an odd shift from 3:30 AM until noon. As a group, they had not worked very much overtime, perhaps a half hour to an hour each day and a few Saturdays, before they volunteered to be laid off.

Usually when autoworkers are first hired into a plant they are assigned a shift. Once in the plant, however, it is possible to request a transfer to another shift, but a worker's ability to obtain such a transfer depends on his or her job classification, seniority, and the particular shift desired. First shift is the most popular among autoworkers for obvious reasons, which means the competition for it is greatest and it is the most difficult to get. An autoworker desiring to work second shift, or third shift if it is available, can often get the shift he or she wants. Sometimes workers are bumped from a shift, for example, from first to second, on the basis of lower seniority. What little control autoworkers have over their work schedule is a product of their ability to request alternative shifts. They can also request transfers to other departments and/or job classifications, and such transfers may be accompanied by a change in shift. Transfers of this nature are granted on the basis of seniority.

The work sharers I spoke with had considerable control of their time while laid off, but they had relatively little control of their time when they were working. Their work schedules existed within a rigid shift system organized around the operation of the assembly line. Not only did the line set the pace of work under a system of technical labor control, but it also established work schedules in the plant and, therefore, was a dominating force in the temporal rhythm of workers' lives.[9] This explains, at least in part, why the work sharers embraced the opportunity to have an extended period of time off the job with such enthusiasm. The layoff was a temporary respite from the rigid work schedules and the repetitive work in the auto plant. It was something many of the work sharers believed they deserved and earned in exchange for long years of service to the company. Not having to go to work, and the consequent removal of the work schedule as a temporal constraint to constantly attend to, was a real source of freedom for them.

Work Sharing and Time Off the Job

How did the work sharers use their time off the job? To begin to answer this question, I must reiterate that the work sharers had volunteered to be laid off, had selected the duration of the layoff, and were assured that they would return to a job at the end of the layoff period. These factors made the work sharers quite distinct from the ordinary laid-off worker who does not volunteer to be laid off, does not determine the duration of the layoff (indeed, it may be indefinite), and is not assured of returning to a job with the same employer. Nor is he/she guaranteed of finding a comparable job with another employer. In addition, the ordinary laid off worker may not be eligible to receive unemployment insurance benefits or the duration of layoff may exceed the period of eligibility.

It is a mistake, however, to assume that the work sharers were carefree during the period of layoff. Those who took the layoff as a trial retirement carefully scrutinized their experiences to determine if their futures should be anticipated with joyous expectation or dread. Those at mid-career were concerned about the health of the domestic automobile industry and their plant's future. They would return to a job at the end of the layoff, but they were uncertain their jobs would extend beyond a few years. Although the work sharers volunteered to be laid off and, for the most part, enjoyed their time off, the fact that workers had to be laid off at all, under any terms, was an indication of serious production problems at the plant.

Despite these concerns, however, the work sharers were the most secure financially of all of the groups of workers I interviewed. They had been paid well as automobile workers for many years, their wages were high because they had high seniority, they were drawing unemployment insurance and supplemental unemployment benefits while laid off, and some shared a household with a second earner.

The zest with which these autoworkers embraced their time off is a measure of the sharp contrast between their experience of time while laid off and employed. One man in particular captured the essence of the self-management of time when he told me how he perceived the difference between being laid off and working full-time:

> General Motors don't govern my time. I'm my own governor. That's what the difference is. Not that I have that much more time. Because I don't because I usually, even now I usually don't get started until two o'clock in the afternoon, but it is still my time. I don't have to worry about getting up and going in to work. It makes a big difference.

The work sharers' use of time off the job reflected, to some degree, the social characteristics of this group. This group was composed disproportionately of middle-aged men. While the majority of this group was married, a higher proportion of individuals in this category was divorced by comparison to those in the groups previously discussed. Their gender, age, and, in some cases, divorced status intersected to free them from child care and other immediate family responsibilities and gave them more time for recreational activities in particular. Some of the work sharers, however, used their extended time off the job to catch up on household work, rekindle neglected interpersonal relationships, and provide service to the community.

Household Projects

Several of the men told me about various "projects" that they were working on. By speaking of their projects, men differentiate their household responsibilities from women's household work, the latter commonly labeled and devalued as "housework." Repeatedly, the men said that their projects required large blocks of time, and they appreciated having such blocks of time while they were laid off. This differs from the temporal shifting of household work that the job-sharing women talked about. In part, this difference reflects differences in the availability of time. The job sharers had a few days or a week off the job at a time, while the work sharers had months off. More important, however, is the relationship between gender and type of household work. Women tend to be responsible for "smaller," less time-consuming tasks (taken individually), but tasks that are done frequently and repeatedly within a short period of time, for example, cooking, washing dishes, dusting, vacuuming, laundry, making beds, and shopping. Many of these tasks need not be discrete. Instead, they may overlap one another such that a woman's "small" tasks shade into one another. She may, therefore, devote considerable time to doing several household tasks in a complex layering of activity. Men, on the other hand, tend to be responsible for tasks that require more time to complete but are done less frequently, such as lawn mowing, automobile repair, and home maintenance. Men's household projects require larger blocks of time to complete; women's household work is more easily adapted to varied parcels of time by fragmenting or bundling tasks.

Mike Sullivan, a self-described night owl, had worked second shift for the entire nineteen years he had worked in the plant. Although his mornings were usually free, they were of insufficient time to complete some of the maintenance projects that had backed up by the time he was laid off. His time on the layoff was an opportunity to catch up on some of these projects. "You know how you always got these projects you want to do when you're working, but you can't do them?" Mike had asked me when we spoke. "Well, I made a list when I got laid off. I put on my coveralls and I took care of a bunch of stuff I wanted to do for myself, my own stuff." Mike's stuff included three off-road machines that he "really wasn't using," and an old, rusted Cadillac. He cleaned and repaired the off-road machines to sell them and pay off his loans, and he sanded out the rust spots on his old Cadillac and had it painted and tuned up. He "took care of all that stuff that piles up when you're working."

Mike explained to me how working full-time had been a disincentive to doing time-consuming household projects. His work schedule interrupted the time necessary to complete them.

> When you're working, like I work second shift, when I get up in the morning, it's hard to start a project because you're not gonna get it done. You have to drop your tools and leave things setting around and go to work. So you don't start those projects. Now that I got all day every day, it's easy to start something and get it done. Because you can stick to it.

For Paul Young, who worked first shift, the main disadvantage of working full-time was that he felt very tired in the evening and could not muster the energy to work on his household projects then. So he put them off and worked himself "to a frazzle" to try to complete them on weekends. Paul was spending his time on the inverse layoff catching up on "all the little jobs" that he was too tired to do when he was working. He spread his household work over several days, and he did not have to rush to try to complete projects in small parcels of time. "I feel better because I know that Saturday rolls around, I don't have to put everything into two days. I can spread it out," he told me. "I used to, if I get up on Saturday morning, have to do something. I'd work myself to a frazzle to get it done. Saturday night would roll around, I was on the couch sleeping. Since I've been laid off, I do just as much but I can spread it out over whenever I want to do it," he explained.

Interpersonal Relationships

A few of the work sharers I met were using their time on the inverse layoff to revitalize neglected relationships with spouses or extended family members. Others used their newfound free time to help relatives and friends in ways that they had been unable to when they worked full-time.

Perhaps the most interesting case I met in this category of use of time off the job was Mary Ellis. Mary had worked fourteen years in the plant, as had her husband. They were the parents of a four-year-old daughter when I spoke with Mary. Mary and her husband had arranged to work split shifts when their daughter was born to share her care. Mary worked days and her husband, Tim, worked second shift. While this arrangement prevented them from having to take their daughter to a day-care center and saved them money as well, it damaged their relationship. As Mary told me, they saw so little of one another on a daily basis that they only had time to "trade troubles." They had virtually no positive time together. They were separated and on the brink of divorce when the inverse layoff scheme was created. Mary volunteered for the layoff, and she convinced her husband to do so, to save her failing marriage. Unfortunately Tim was unwilling to speak with me, but Mary confided that she believed the layoff probably saved their marriage. It gave them time to be together, to talk about their problems, and to develop strategies for revitalizing their marriage. They did simple things like going out to breakfast together, something they had not done since before their daughter was born. They took hikes together. In Mary's words, "everyday was Saturday." Mary also developed a new relationship with her daughter. Since Mary had worked days, she had missed her daughter's daytime activities. She did not know, for example, her daughter's breakfast routine. Getting to know her daughter more completely was like a voyage of discovery for Mary, an adventure that had been facilitated by the inverse layoff.

To avoid the difficulties of the split shift arrangement, Mary and Tim Ellis had agreed that both would work first shift when they returned to their jobs after the layoff. Their daughter would go to a day-care facility until she was enrolled in school. Mary, in particular, believed this new arrangement would make them a more conventional family because they would be home together each evening, and she hoped this new arrangement would become the foundation for a more solid relationship.

Paul Young had been married twenty years. Although his relationship with his wife was in no way as fragile as that of the Ellises, work-induced fatigue had led Paul to spend less energy on his marriage. As Paul explained to me, "It's very hard to communicate. Like me, you get off work, you don't feel like doing nothing. You go home and set down and have supper, you don't feel like going anywhere." But now that Paul had "the time and the patience" during his extended time off, he had reclaimed the day and rejuvenated his relationship with his wife. By being home during the day, he shared her world. Because he was not working at his physically taxing job, he had the energy and desire to go places with her and talk with her. They went out for breakfast or lunch once or twice a week. By spending this time together in the absence of their son, who was in school, they were nurturing and strenghtening a relationship that had languished.

One cannot assume, however, that work time reduction fosters better interpersonal relationships. Kevin Connelly, a man in his early thirties (with about fifteen years of seniority in the plant) and the father of two young children, for example, complained that he and his wife were not getting along as well as they used to. While he acknowledged that the tension between them may stem from many different sources, he wondered whether the fact that they had more time together had exaggerated the difficulties in their relationship. "We're not used to seeing each other that much," Kevin explained. "Our differences are showing up more."

In addition to dealing with deep emotional entanglements during the period of layoff, some of the work sharers used their time to help others, thereby nurturing interpersonal relationships of a different sort. Dave Reed, for example, ran errands for his mother, and Mike Sullivan helped a friend's father build an addition onto his home. Paul Young helped his brother install a kitchen in the basement for his wife's cake-baking business. Carl Szabo helped friends remodel their house, repaired his niece's car, and helped a friend with some repairs at his store. In most of these examples, the projects were sufficiently time-consuming that the men would not have offered their help had they been working full-time.

Ideally, helping is altruistic, noncompetitive, and the basis of reciprocal exchange. It is also a form of nonmarket exchange. Helpers feel good about themselves because they give something—time and service—to others. Helping integrates people with others and solidifies relationships. Mutual expressions of need and support deepen a sense of commitment and trust among people. Yet helping may become a low priority for people who feel that they have little time to give. Their time is already spread thin over more immediate obligations; they have little surplus to use to reach out to others. When the work schedule is removed as one constraint on time, however, individuals may become more generous in their offers of help to others. A similar generosity may also characterize community participation. By participating in the larger community, individuals extend their helpfulness beyond their immediate network of kin and friends. Altruistic deeds extend to virtual strangers, converting those strangers to friends. Such is the fabric of community.

Community Service

A number of the work sharers I spoke with were using their time to continue or increase participation in community activities. Paul Young and John Olson were active participants in their church. Their involvement was not new—they had been active members when they worked full-time—but it was extended in time and substance while they were laid off. Paul, for example, increased the amount of time he devoted to preparing for a class on the Bible that he taught one night each week. When he worked full-time, he could only devote a few hours to preparation for the class. While laid off he had more time to read and do research for the class, starting several days in advance, and he believed the quality of his instruction had improved since he had more time to devote to preparation. John Olson attended several church meetings in the evening during the week, which he had done for a long time. On the layoff he also spent time during the day at the church, doing maintenance like replacing the roof, cutting down a tree, and mowing the lawn.

Like the job-sharing mothers who volunteered in the schools and served as scout troop leaders, Paul Young accompanied his son's Cub Scout troop on nature hikes and participated in a five-man rotation of coaches and umpires for his son's baseball games. Such participation was Paul's effort to be involved in his son's life and to develop a closeness he thought lacking in most father-son relationships and that he had missed with his own father. Paul's own father had driven himself hard to "work, work, work," so that he was often exhausted when he was at home. He had little energy for any activities other than sleeping in a chair and watching television. He was emotionally withdrawn from his family. Paul strove to be a different kind of father, and his participation in Cub Scouts and with his son's baseball team were opportunities to fulfill his ideal of fatherhood.

Ted McKinley spoke eloquently about his community service. He had begun to work with a substance abuse program some time before he was laid off. He had become so invested in the program that sometimes it interfered with his job, leading to disciplinary action on a few occasions. On the inverse layoff, Ted devoted most of his time to his volunteer work. He derived considerable satisfaction from that volunteer work and likened it to "giving something to myself that I had never been able to do." He enjoyed helping people in trouble and often would stay at the center all night, until six or seven o'clock in the morning, just to talk to someone having a difficult time. His volunteer experience with the substance abuse program had increased the value of interpersonal relationships in Ted's life. As he explained to me,

> I never had time before. It used to be you'd run into an old friend, you get a few minutes to talk with him, you're on your way to work or somewhere. Now I can say, 'well, I'm on my way to nowhere, and there ain't nothing that's so important happening to me today that I can't postpone it' and sit down and talk to an old friend, or even a new friend. I really enjoy that. That alone could be more than adequate to offset any economic loss that I gave up when I took this inverse.

Another work sharer, however, had developed an interest in a new community service activity during the inverse layoff but remained reluctant to pursue it. Sharon Rogers had offered support and assistance to a friend who was terminally ill with cancer. Sharon found the experience so rewarding and gratifying that she thought she might like to become a hospice volunteer. Her reluctance to do so was explained by the fact that Sharon would eventually return to her full-time auto job. She believed the nature of the service she wanted to provide to those in need required continued involvement and deep commitment that would be interrupted by her job once she returned to it. Sharon preferred not to volunteer at all rather than start an activity on which she could not follow through.

Sharon's situation illustrates the way in which full-time employment can curb community participation even among those persons with a strong desire to engage in community service. The full-time work schedule, the inability to control that schedule, and the fatigue that usually accompanies full-time employment interfere with people's ability to commit and follow through. Individuals who want to participate in community activities but believe they cannot cut off a part of themselves, becoming more unidimensional than they would prefer to be. As a result, their spirits may suffer. And the community suffers, too, because it loses the contributions of civic-minded persons whose involvement would most assuredly enrich the community.

Recreation

The work sharers pursued recreational activities similar to those mentioned in previous chapters, such as spectator sports, leisure sports such as golf and jogging, exercise at health clubs, walking, gardening, and knitting. But because this group is disproportionately composed of men, some of their recreational interests were traditionally masculine in nature. Several men in this group told me about hunting, camping, and fishing trips they had enjoyed. What is distinctive about these forms of recreation is that they occur away from home, and they presuppose the ability, or freedom, to be away from home. Men who took such trips were free to do so, at least in part because their children were grown, they had no children, they were divorced without child care responsibilities, or their wives ordinarily tended to the children so the father's absence from the home did not interfere with their care. These trips were usually made by men alone or in the company of other men. Women and children rarely accompanied them.

A couple of the work sharers owned cottages or trailers near their favorite recreational sites. Peter Garcia liked to spend perhaps two weeks at a time at his cottage where he could fish and enjoy the outdoors. For him in particular, the inverse layoff was advantageous because he was not limited to weekend fishing trips, short, sweet, and irritating because he was on the road with hordes of others making similar weekend getaways. On the inverse, Peter could travel during the week and stay longer than a few days if he so chose. Bob Martin had actually moved into his trailer at his favorite campsite, returning to town once a week or so for brief periods of time to check on his home and take care of personal matters. He intended to live in his trailer throughout the autumn months until the Michigan winter would make it unliveable. Then, he thought, he would go to Florida.

It is these types of recreational pursuits that underline the vacation-like quality of the inverse layoff. Among those who could afford to do so and who also had few constraints at home, the inverse layoff became not only a break from the job but also an opportunity to get away from the usual daily routines of home.

In sum, a number of the work sharers used their time off the job to work on household projects, particularly to catch up on projects that had been put off when they were working. A few used their new-found time to revitalize interpersonal relationships that had languished over time. Some used their time to engage in community service or their favorite recreational activities.

Summary and Conclusion

The work sharers I met had volunteered to be laid off temporarily under an inverse seniority layoff scheme. Layoff under the inverse seniority scheme was a temporary respite for high-seniority autoworkers from the rigidity of the work schedule and the monotony of work in the auto plant. Extended time off the job was an opportunity for workers nearing retirement to ease into retirement. Other workers had more time to work on household projects, to rekindle interpersonal relationships, to commit to community service, and to engage in personally satisfying recreational activities. The relative economic security of the work sharers contrasts in particular with the insecurity of intermittently employed temporaries (discussed in chapter five) who had so few placements that they were effectively unemployed, although they were not drawing unemployment insurance benefits. For such temporaries, free time, even if it is passed in enjoyable ways, may be worrisome and anxiety-provoking because they would rather be working and earning more income. Their limited discretionary income also restricts the off-the-job activities in which they can choose to participate. Unlike these temporaries, the work sharers, who *were* technically unemployed, seemed to be free of such financial worries. With unemployment insurance and supplemental unemployment benefits, the work sharers received about 90 percent of their straight-time pay, despite being laid off. They were also secure in the knowledge that they would return to a job at the end of the layoff period. With few financial or job worries, the work sharers were essentially "on vacation," enjoying household projects, interpersonal relationships, community service, and recreational activities. Only a few were plagued by the uncertain future of the domestic automobile industry or their distaste for factory work. These individuals used some of their time off to consider alternative employment.

Chapter Eight

The Promise and Limits of Reduced Work

In this book I have explored four different types of reduced work: conventional part-time employment, temporary employment, job sharing, and work sharing under an inverse seniority layoff scheme. I have also explored individuals' reasons for participating in these varied forms of reduced work and their use of time off the job. I have argued that reduced work exists within a larger social complex of post-industrialism, gender relations, and labor market segmentation. This social context influences the nature of reduced work as well as the use of gendered labor in reduced-work situations. Reduced work in turn has implications for work schedules, income, and job security, thereby influencing to some degree use of time off the job. Women and men tend to use their time off the job differently, so gender is also an analytic factor at this micro level. In this chapter I summarize the implications of reduced work for personal autonomy and quality of life among women and men.

Four Types of Reduced Work Compared

Among conventional part-time workers, the quality of life depends on the nature of the work schedule and the amount of control the worker has over the schedule. Some part-time workers have regular schedules. They know from week to week what hours they must be on the job whether they control their schedule or not. This regularity makes the schedule predictable and facilitates planning for the individual. If the worker does not control the schedule, however, it may still interfere with other activities the worker would like to pursue because work hours are scheduled at the wrong time. If the schedule breaks time off the job into too many small fragments, certain activities may be forgone because such fragmentation precludes participation in them. Irregular schedules, by contrast, are highly unpredictable unless the worker controls his or her schedule. This unpredictability interferes with the ability to make commitments, therefore part-time workers tend to use their time off the job engaged in activities that can be undertaken spontaneously and molded to the available time. Household work is the most common activity of this sort. These part-time workers may experience social isolation because of the unpredictability of their schedule.

The nature of the schedule, combined with level of pay, further influences the part-time worker's quality of life. Many conventional part-time jobs pay relatively low wages, thus part-time workers often find themselves with little discretionary income. The lack of discretionary income to use for recreational purposes in particular may further isolate the part-time worker. Such workers may actually lead work-centered lives, making themselves always available to work whenever their employer might need them because they want to earn more income. They avoid committing themselves to other activities because they want to be free to work.

These generalities regarding part-time workers pertain to both women and men, although it is more likely that women work part-time to integrate wage work and child care. In this case women may not seek additional hours of employment because more hours would interfere with their ability to spend time with their children. When women are employed part-time to balance wage work and child care, they are most often married and their husband is the primary earner in the home. The availability of alternative support permits women to use part-time employment to their advantage, although their child care and household responsibilities may prevent them from pursuing an array of off-the-job activities they might enjoy, particularly if their husbands do not share these responsibilities with them. Part-time employment for many women, therefore, continues to be an accommodation to dual spheres of responsibility and reinforces the traditional gender division of labor in our society.

The same cannot be said about temporary employment largely because none of the individuals I spoke with used temporary employment to integrate wage work and household responsibilities. Temporary employment is far too unpredictable to attempt to mesh it with child care in particular. How can one plan adequately for a child's substitute care if one does not know whether and when one will be employed? Part-time workers on irregular schedules might face the same problem.

Some temporaries are fortunate to hold placements steadily over the period of several weeks or months. Their hours may be part-time or full-time, but they work these hours consistently over a relatively long period of time. They may work at the same site or at different sites during this time. These temporaries maximize their earnings, although they may complain of limited free time and little discretionary income because wages paid to temporaries are often low. Because the placement is expected to be finite, temporary workers may prefer to save rather than spend whatever discretionary income they earn in anticipation of a period of unemployment when the placement is terminated.

Temporaries whose placements are intermittent face long periods of unemployment between placements of relatively short duration. They may attempt to supplement their income from temporary employment by working in the informal economy. They, too, have work-centered lives despite large amounts of free time because they are ever needful of income. They are always looking for opportunities to earn money.

The exception, of course, is the temporary with alternative sources of financial support, whether that be a spouse or a parent. Individuals with such alternative support can ride out periods of unemployment more readily than those without such support.

Job sharing appears to be a uniformly superior form of reduced work by comparison to conventional part-time employment and temporary employment because the jobs held by job sharers tend to be more secure. Most of the job sharers I spoke with had been employed full-time for several years before sharing a job. Job sharing was an effort on their part to continue career involvement, but they wanted to work reduced hours to accommodate some off-the-job activity, usually child care. As a group, the job sharers earned wages considerably higher than the conventional part-time and temporary employees. Most were married as well, and the loss of income from job sharing was readily absorbed because the spouse was also employed, usually full-time.

By comparison to conventional part-time and temporary employment, job sharing provides workers with greater opportunities to control their work schedule. Job sharers, thus, can negotiate a schedule with their job-share partner and supervisors that optimizes their participation in a myriad of activities.

Job sharers are overwhelmingly women, underlining the employment option as an accommodation to child care and household responsibilities. The women I spoke with reported spending most of their time off the job engaged in these activities. Some also found time for recreation or community service, particularly if the gender politics in their home were such that they could claim such autonomous time. Like conventional part-time employment, however, job sharing reinforces the traditional gender division of labor because women use it to balance dual spheres of responsibility.

The single most important distinguishing feature of the group of work sharers I met, by contrast to the conventional part-time workers, the temporaries, and the job sharers, is that it is disproportionately made up of men. This is explained by the industrial setting within which the work-sharing scheme I studied occurred. The work sharers were high-seniority automobile workers who volunteered to be laid off temporarily under an inverse seniority layoff plan. Manufacturing generally, and automobile manufacturing in particular, tends to employ large numbers of men and relatively few women, particularly in production jobs.

The industrial sector in this case has ramifications for workers' earnings and the terms and conditions of the inverse layoff. Automobile workers are among the highest paid hourly workers in the United States; that combined with high seniority made the work sharers the highest paid group in my sample. Under the work sharing plan, workers received unemployment insurance benefits and supplemental unemployment benefits while laid off. These benefits amounted to about 90 percent of their regular straight-time pay. Unlike the conventional part-time workers and the temporaries, financial worries were not prominent among the work sharers with whom I spoke.

The work sharers were essentially on extended vacation. They used their time to complete household projects, to revitalize neglected interpersonal relationships, to participate in community service, and to engage in recreational activities they enjoyed. They embraced the opportunity for extended time off as a respite from the rigid work schedules and monotonous work associated with work on the assembly line. Unlike workers laid off indefinitely, the work sharers were secure in the knowledge that they would return to a job at the end of the inverse layoff period. While the relative ill health of the domestic automobile industry was a concern, most had sufficient seniority so as not to fear for their jobs. They would at least be assured of transfer rights should their plant close.

Gender and Reduced Work Reconsidered

Gender comparisons within categories of reduced work are meaningful, but comparisons across categories may be most telling. French social critic André Gorz has argued that women are the vanguard of a post-industrial, post-employment revolution, rejecting the "productivist ethic" for time spent in nurturing relations with others.[1] The female job sharers and some part-time workers with whom I spoke certainly made this choice, but are they pioneers forging the way to a new society or are they trapped by contradictions in the present? As much as I would like to believe the former, it is difficult not to be skeptical. With prevailing definitions of gender giving primary responsibility for child care to women, are women who choose to work less than full-time at a wage-paying job actively rejecting a productivist ethic or are they simply doing what they are supposed to do as women? Feminist values emphasizing nurturance and care have certainly gained a foothold in the society, but they remain politically contested and they are far from hegemonic. Given this political culture, are women who work less than full-time a revolutionary vanguard or misfits in a culture that values full-time wage work? As some of the job sharers with whom I spoke noted, they had to struggle to obtain their job-share arrangements, and some were stigmatized or demoted for winning this dubious privilege. This does not strike me as a group around which others are likely to rally. Their relative powerlessness and lack of organization render them ineffectual as leaders despite the apparent progressivism of their job-sharing experiments.

But the job sharers I spoke with, despite areas of vulnerability, were protected somewhat from supervisory caprice by civil service employment regulations and labor union representation. This accords them relatively more power than many conventional part-time and temporary workers. Part-time workers and temporaries remain most vulnerable to the vicissitude of the market, and without union protection they have little power to guard their positions as workers. The work sharers are perhaps the most powerful of the four groups I met. Despite the vulnerability of those at mid-career who might have faced job loss in the not-too-distant future, their jobs were protected as were their incomes and benefits during the period of voluntary temporary layoff. True, the UAW has lost membership and strength as a result of the automobile industry's restructuring, but the UAW remains one of the most powerful unions in the nation and rests on a foundation of hard-won rights for workers. There is a safety net in place for the autoworkers that simply does not exist for most conventional part-time and temporary workers. Perhaps the work sharers are the post-employment vanguard for they have refused socialized labor—at least for the period of time they volunteered to be laid off—and they represent a legacy of union struggle that has gained benefits approximating a social income of the sort Gorz envisions.[2] Yet they are far from a feminist vanguard and, therefore, unlikely to lead us to Gorz's post-industrial future.

Gorz asserts that the "post-industrial neo-proletariat" defines its own subjectivity through the refusal of socialized labor and implies that this refusal is motivated by work-based alienation.[3] He states, "...neo-proletarians are basically non-workers temporarily doing something that means nothing to them."[4] In turn, this post-industrial neo-proletariat seeks to appropriate areas of autonomy outside and in opposition to the logic of capitalist society for purposes of individual development.[5]

The work sharers I met expressed evidence of worker alienation when they discussed the routine and monotonous nature of their jobs and when they expressed hostility toward General Motors for actions the corporation had taken in its reorganization efforts. Their volunteering for the inverse layoff was an act of refusal of socialized labor. While a few part-time workers and temporaries preferred reduced work because they valued their time off the job, many wanted regular, steady, full-time employment because they needed the income. In those cases, reduced work did not represent a refusal of socialized labor so much as making do with contingent work because that is all that was available. And in cases where individuals worked forty-hour weeks as part-time and temporary workers, their work schedules inhibited their ability to appropriate areas of autonomy, even if they were so inclined. The female job sharers' refusal of socialized labor was not the product of worker alienation but gender-related responsibilities rooted in social definitions of motherhood, although clerical jobs can indeed be routine and child care is a socially appropriate reason for women to work less than full-time—a reason that women may use to mask dissatisfaction with a routine job. Yet the job-sharing women I met seemed to value their wage-paying jobs. Employment was a source of identity and autonomy because it gave them an income and a public role in a society that values wage-paying work more than privatized, unpaid work.

The differences in pay, benefits, and employment security among the people with whom I spoke reflect differences in reduced work in various labor market segments. Those employed in manufacturing are the beneficiaries of what remains of the post-World War II capital-labor accord when increases in productivity were passed on to workers in the form of higher wages and benefits. Those employed in the public sector, principally the job sharers in this study, are the beneficiaries of wage determination practices that link the public sector to wage levels in the unionized private sector. But part-time workers, particularly those without union representation, and temporary employees make a precarious living at best.

The state could certainly establish policy to minimize the effects of labor market segmentation by mandating an increase in the minimum wage and requiring employers to provide benefits to their part-time and temporary workers. Recently a modest increase in the minimum wage was enacted, but mandated benefits seem unlikely, given that employers use part-time and temporary workers in part to avoid paying benefits. Such a public policy, however, would be consistent with Gorz's vision of the administrative state in the post-industrial future. Following Marx, Gorz sees two key functions of the state: to ensure that everyone has the necessities of life and to define the amount of socially necessary labor required from each individual. Yet these coordinating activities of the state must be performed at the same time that its powers of domination are abolished and it checks the ability of classes or groups in society to dominate other groups. By executing its responsibility to define and allocate socially necessary labor time but doing so with restricted power, the state avoids *imposing* work time reduction and increased free time on individuals. Instead, people are empowered to take more free time if they want it.[6] But to ensure that gender asymmetries in free time do not persist, thereby checking the power of men to dominate women, Gorz's administrative state would have to incorporate nurturing work, like child, dependent, and elder care, into its definition of socially necessary labor and monitor the distribution of this work across women and men. Whether such oversight is anti-democratic, and therefore inconsistent with Gorz's otherwise egalitarian vision, is, of course, another question.

So far, the state has not taken an active role in promoting the redistribution of wage work through work time reduction, except with regard to short-time compensation. On both the federal and state levels there persists faith in the ability of the economy to grow and generate jobs, although strategies for stimulating economic growth vary from state to state and between state and federal government. As noted in chapter one, the last time the federal government wrestled with the issue of generalized work time reduction was in the late 1970s after U.S. Representative John Conyers (D-Michigan) introduced legislation to amend the Fair Labor Standards Act by reducing the standard workweek to thirty-five hours, increasing premium pay for overtime, and eliminating mandatory overtime. At that time, proponents argued that a generalized reduction of the workweek would decrease unemployment and offset the social costs of unemployment; combat technological unemployment; relieve stress on the job, thereby improving morale and productivity; decrease absenteeism; and improve the quality of life off the job. They believed it could also help conserve energy if work time reduction decreased commuting and permitted buildings to be closed part of each week. By employing more people, income tax revenues would increase as would net consumption demand. Opponents, however, believed generalized work time reduction would increase labor costs and bring about a decline in productivity if unqualified persons were employed. It would be inflationary because increased labor costs would lead to an increase in prices which, paradoxically, might exacerbate unemployment in the long run if employers tried to offset higher labor costs with increased mechanization. Further, a reduction of the workweek would increase multiple job holding, and a legislated reduction, they believed, would interfere with the operation of the collective bargaining system.[7] Economists generally criticize efforts to reduce the workweek because such efforts assume the amount of work in a society is fixed. They argue that the amount of work can be increased if the economy expands.[8] The political contest over reduction of the workweek reached a stalemate; the bill never progressed beyond committee hearings.[9]

The principal strategy to promote economic growth adopted by the Reagan and Bush administrations has been tax reduction to stimulate investment. What support for work time reduction exists at the federal and state levels encourages experimentation with short-time and flexible-time options among public-sector employees. Such policy seems particularly responsive to the needs of female employees, but it also threatens to marginalize them in a "mommy track."[10] Clearly, government lacks any comprehensive time policy in its efforts to manage economic transition.

But issues and conflicts around time will persist—if not because of underemployment and slow economic growth, then because women will continue to be active participants in the paid labor force. We as a society must face the fact that the 1950s "cult of domesticity" no longer exists, and our social institutions must be altered to reflect that fact.[11] Employers must become more responsive to the needs of working parents. This might include a redefinition of the full-time workweek from the normative forty hours a week (8:00 AM to 5:00 PM, Monday through Friday in most offices) to 9:00 AM to 3:00 PM, Monday through Friday to coincide with the hours children are in school.[12] Flexible hours should be available to the parents of preschool-age children and those who do not want to work full-time. Work on weekends, during the evening hours, and at night should be optional (which means some businesses may be forced to close during those hours if they cannot get employees to work then). Employer-provided benefits might include on-site child care and/or child care allowances to pay part of the cost of child care as well as paid parental leaves for parents of new infants and ill children. Dependent care coverage might be an option available to employees caring for aging and ailing parents. These benefits could be supplements to or substitutes for publicly provided child and dependent care. While a feminist conception of full-time employment and employer-provided benefits does not address the problem of gender asymmetries in household work and caregiving, it may be a step in the right direction if it applies equally to women and men, thus encouraging men to take on more of the responsibility of nurturing work.

Reduced Work and Community

A final set of theoretical questions arises from the analysis of reduced work, personal autonomy, and gender developed in this book. These questions have to do with the relationship between reduced work and community service. Could reduced work foster reconstruction and renewal of community? Is this even desirable? While my interviews provide an inconclusive answer to the first question, they suggest that reduced work might foster greater community participation under certain kinds of conditions. Reduced work facilitates such participation when work schedules are predictable and when they do not perpetuate the tyranny of the forty-hour week. With sufficient free time, and some knowledge of when one must be at work, individuals can make the kinds of commitments necessary to engage in community service on an ongoing basis. In the absence of such free time, either because the hours of employment are too long or other responsibilities interfere, and when the work schedule is unpredictable, individuals so inclined may be prevented from participating in community service. Because voluntary associations can be spheres of democratic participation, reduced work should be organized to permit sufficient time for individuals who wish to do so to participate in community activities. If the work schedule must be irregular, it should be under the worker's control as much as possible to facilitate the integration of wage work with off-the-job pursuits such as community service.

But is greater community participation desirable? Should we be concerned if citizens do not participate in political and community affairs as much as they might? To answer these questions, I defer to the authors of the widely acclaimed book, *Habits of the Heart*. They argue that one of the keys to the survival of democratic institutions is the relationship between private and public life, the way in which individuals do, or do not, participate in public life. If this is true, participation in local politics and sustained connection to the wider political community support the maintenance of democratic institutions.[13]

But are there temporal limits to community participation? To what extent does employment create temporal limits to community participation? Marxists, of course, have noted contradictory forces associated with employment in capitalist society. On the one hand, labor is increasingly socialized. The wage-labor system draws individuals into socialized workplaces, creating the basis of collectivization and unity among workers. Yet competition for jobs divides workers, as do divisions based on race, ethnicity, religion, age, and gender, and subordination by employers prevents workers' collective power from coming to full flower. Market forces atomize individuals, too, particularly through the production of goods for personal use. Today many people in the United States drive to work alone, drive home alone, watch television by themselves, if they live alone, or retire to a room by themselves to watch a program different from that being watched by the rest of the household on one of the two or three television sets the household owns. Individuals go for walks or ride bikes, wired to personal headsets, locked in a private world of sound disconnected from others. The lines of food items conveniently packaged for singles increase in number as the number of singles in the population continues to grow. This proliferation of items for personal consumption enhances profits because individual units generally sell at higher prices than bulk. While this Marxist analysis provides some insight into the possibilities for and obstacles to community participation in capitalist society, it does not say anything about the temporal limits of work with regard to community participation.

Today individuals who are employed full-time spend approximately half of their waking hours on the job. Commuting to and from the job may add as much as an hour or two to the length of the workday in many large cities and for those who commute from rural to urban areas. Much of time off the job is devoted to personal care activities, household work, child care, and the like. Recreational activities are squeezed in when it is possible to find the time. Some individuals make time to attend church regularly. Political participation is virtually non-existent for the vast majority.[14] Reduced work hours provide more time for non-job activities in theory, but the practice suggests greater community participation is related to the timing and control of hours of employment, even when employment is less than full-time.

Political theorist Alan Wolfe has argued that capitalist society gives rise to alienated politics in the form of the state. The state extracts power from people and, in turn, imposes that alien power on them. The state is an illusory community.[15] Depending on the extent of participation and the nature of the issues around which participation occurs, community participation may permit people to reclaim some of the power expropriated by the state. While voluntary associations may be conservative forces in society, reinforcing the status quo, they can be the organizational base from which grow movements for progressive social change. The church in the African-American community played this organizational role in the civil rights movement in the United States. Conservative or progressive, voluntary associations provide opportunities for autonomous citizen participation and political education.[16] Such community participation takes time and requires sustained commitment. Individuals whose employment creates a lack of time or inhibits commitment most likely will not be active participants in communitarian projects despite the will to participate.

Sirianni has argued that time scarcity undermines rational political decision making. Urgency takes priority over importance, and time is fragmented into periods too brief for adequate reflection and political deliberation. Meeting deadlines becomes more important than making decisions consistent with a preferred system of values. Participation and consensus formation are restricted by practical considerations of time scarcity. A new economy of time, he believes, could provide time for genuine public activity and political participation.[17]

Reduced work may be a step toward this new economy of time, but only in certain forms and under certain conditions. Reduced work that is irregular, with schedules under an employer's control, may preclude individuals' community participation despite the absolute availability of time because workers cannot make commitments from week to week. Reduced work that is an accommodation to child care may limit community participation to the extent that child care interferes with such participation, although parenthood can create opportunities for participation as well. Reduced work that provides inadequate remuneration to workers may inhibit community participation since these individuals avoid such participation to make themselves ever available for employment.

Currently, two models of relation and community seem to be on the rise, neither of which fulfills the vision of community participation suggested here. The first, which I call the corporate model, places the corporation at the center of community and equates the corporation with the community. This is advocated by neo-liberal writers, such as Robert B. Reich, who want to borrow Japanese corporate practices and apply them in the United States. This includes making the corporation a deliverer of social services. Reich promotes a dismantling of the welfare state and transfer of its responsibilities to corporations. This model extends the power and domination of capital even further into the sphere of community, thus threatening community autonomy. Reich has an answer to this: workers control corporate welfare programs, thereby differentiating his proposal from the welfare capitalism of the early twentieth century. But this is insufficient given that even worker-controlled corporate welfare programs would remain hostage to the vicissitude of the profit motive and hierarchical corporate relations. Corporate control of workers could increase under this model if workers' social safety net is attached to their performance as workers.[18]

Another manifestation of the corporate model of community comes in the guise of corporate health and recreation programs for workers. This is exemplified by those companies that provide such perquisites as tennis courts and aerobics classes for their employees. Although I do not mean to dismiss any humanitarian motives on the part of companies in providing such programs, the primary rationale behind them is cost efficiency. Corporations today bear a major burden in health care costs for their insured employees, and promoting healthy lifestyles might be a strategy to reduce the costs of health insurance that employers pay. If such health and exercise programs relieve worker stress, workers may be more productive in the long run, thereby advantaging the employer.

I have no objections to healthy living, but I do object to corporate-dominated models of community. As stated previously, employees who use these services remain subordinate to the interests of the corporation. Further, not all workers in the society are or will be attached to corporate employers, and they would be excluded from the corporate community. Few small businesses can afford to develop recreation programs of the sort just described or provide social welfare programs to their employees.

The second model of relation and community which is on the rise today is the therapeutic model. Therapy is part and parcel of the quest for relation and community in an increasingly individualistic society. The therapist may be a substitute for significant others missing in one's life or may (the client hopes) provide assistance in finding relation and community. Adelmann recently has documented the increase in the percentage of Americans who sought mental health care between 1957 and 1976, from 4 to 13 percent. Still a minority of the population, the rate of increase (more than 200 percent in a twenty-year period) reflects, she argues, the greater availability of mental health services and changes in the way Americans think about their own well-being. Cultural changes have also led to increased demand for mental health service. The triumph of individualism over community and geographic separation from extended family contribute to a sense of social isolation for many people. In the absence of adequate social support, they may turn to mental health care professionals when they have personal problems.[19]

Therapy, however, may not be an adequate substitute for significant social bonds. First, the relationship is contractual; and second, it is asymmetrical, focused on the client. Further, it is an unequal relationship circumscribed in time and space by the therapist. In the language of social psychologist, Charles Horton Cooley, the therapeutic relationship is a secondary relationship—an inadequate substitute for the primary relationship for which the client may be searching.

The therapeutic model is also an extension of the value of bourgeois individualism in advanced capitalist society. As such, it tends to focus on individuals as the cause of their own problems and does not entertain social solutions to personal problems. Indeed, therapy itself is a product of advanced capitalism, representing yet further extension of the market into profitable areas of service delivery.[20]

In *Civilization and Its Discontents*, Freud argued that humans require a balance of work and love.[21] Psychologists today continue to trumpet balanced lives for individual well being. Yet it takes time to pursue the varied activities that constitute a balanced life. When we spend most of our waking hours at work, even if it is a job we enjoy, and the rest of our hours recovering and preparing for the next day, or catching up at a feverish pace on household tasks, our lives are necessarily one-sided. The experiences of the people that I spoke with suggest that reduced work can provide the increased time necessary to build balanced lives. But reduced work does not do this by definition, particularly if the work schedule and/or inadequate pay and employment insecurity interfere with one's ability to achieve such balance.

The central question that I have posed in this book has to do with the relationship between reduced work and personal autonomy, or more broadly stated, reduced work and quality of life. I argued that their relationship is complex, that the industrial sector within which reduced work occurs, the type of occupation, the level of pay, the degree of employment security, the work schedule, and the gender of the individual who is employed less than full-time influence personal autonomy and, thus, quality of life. Therefore, it cannot be assumed that reduced work fosters greater personal autonomy or an enriched quality of life, but under certain conditions reduced work is the foundation for "the best of both worlds." I also suggested that reduced work may be a vehicle for the reconstruction of community if it provides individuals with time to commit to community service. Reconstructing community at the local level and building community at the international level may be our most urgent enterprise today. In the nuclear age, our survival as a species depends on it.

Notes

Notes for Chapter One

1. Gayle Rubin defines the sex/gender system as the set of arrangements by which a society transforms biological sexuality into products of human activity and in which these transformed sexual needs are satisfied. It is rooted in a society's system of kinship and reflected in its division of labor by sex. See her classic statement, "The Traffic in Women: Notes on the 'Political Economy' of Sex," in *Toward an Anthropology of Women*, ed. Rayna R. Reiter (New York: Monthly Review Press, 1975).

2. All names are fictitious to protect informants' identities.

3. Fred Best, *Flexible Life Scheduling: Breaking the Education-Work-Retirement Lockstep* (New York: Praeger, 1980).

4. Barry Bluestone and Bennett Harrison, *The Deindustrialization of America* (New York: Basic Books, 1982).

5. Mary Frank Fox and Sharlene Hesse-Biber, *Women at Work* (Palo Alto, CA: Mayfield, 1984).

6. Signed into law on 25 June 1938, by President Franklin D. Roosevelt, to become effective 24 October 1938, the Fair Labor Standards Act (FLSA) has been called the "cornerstone" of federal labor legislation (McGaughey, *A Shorter Workweek*, 252) and has been assessed as "second only to the Social Security Act" in significance (Elder and Miller, 11). The FLSA established the minimum wage, maximum hours, and premium pay for overtime. For accounts of the politics surrounding the formulation and passage of the act, see Orme Wheelock Phelps, *The Legislative Background of the Fair Labor Standards Act* (Chicago: The University of Chicago Press, 1939); Jonathan Grossman, "Fair Labor Standards Act of 1938: Maximum Struggle for a Minimum Wage," *Monthly Labor Review* 101 (June 1978): 22–30; and Ronnie Steinberg, *Wages and Hours: Labor Reform in Twentieth-Century America* (New Brunswick, NJ: Rutgers University Press, 1982). For discussions of the history of the FLSA, particularly its enforcement record and amendments, see Peyton K. Elder and Heidi D. Miller, "The Fair Labor Standards Act: Changes of Four Decades,"

Monthly Labor Review 102 (July 1979): 10–16; and William McGaughey, Jr., *A Shorter Workweek in the 1980s* (White Bear Lake, MN: Thistlerose Publications, 1981), 252–256. For a discussion of the effect of state maximum hours laws and the overtime provisions of the FLSA on women, see Ronnie Steinberg Ratner, "The Paradox of Protection: Maximum Hours Legislation in the United States," *International Labour Review* 119 (March–April 1980): 185–198. On Conyers' effort to amend the act see McGaughey, *A Shorter Workweek*, 254–256.

7. McGaughey, *A Shorter Workweek*, 255; "Factories of the Future: A Shop Floor View," *Dollars and Sense* (September 1985): 8–9, 16.

8. David Moberg, "Service Economy Not Serving U.S.," *In These Times*, 17 May 1989), 2.

9. "Dutch Lesson," *The Economist*, 12 May 1984, 77; "At Last, the 38 1/2-Hour Solution," *The Economist*, 30 June 1984, 58.

10. "Flexiyears," *The Economist*, 5 March 1983, 76.

11. Mary Frank Fox and Sharlene Hesse-Biber, *Women At Work* (Palo Alto, CA: Mayfield Publishing Co., 1984), 35.

12. U.S. Department of Labor, Women's Bureau, *Time of Change: 1983 Handbook on Women Workers* (Washington, DC: Government Printing Office, 1983), 52.

13. Robert W. Bednarzik, "Worksharing in the U.S.: Its Prevalence and Duration," *Monthly Labor Review* 103 (July 1980): 3–12.

14. This argument assumes the division of child care responsibilities between women and men is a matter of the availability of time, not gender. An important flaw in this argument is that the gender division of labor in society determines the availability of time, not vice versa, yet this argument is premised on the logical sequence that the availability of time determines the gender division of labor. The question of the relative effects of gender and available time on time spent in household work is explored further in chapter two.

15. Gretl S. Meier, *Job Sharing: A New Pattern for Quality of Work and Life* (Kalamazoo, MI: W. E. Upjohn Institute for Employment Research, 1979), 58.

16. Carmen Sirianni, "Economies of Time in Social Theory: Three Approaches Compared," *Current Perspectives in Social Theory* 8 (1987): 161–195.

17. Eviatar Zerubavel, "Timetables and Scheduling: On the Social Organization of Time," *Sociological Inquiry* 46 (1976): 87–94.

18. Hilda Kahne, *Reconceiving Part-Time Work: New Perspectives for Older Workers and Women* (Totowa, NJ: Rowman and Allanheld, 1985).

19. Ibid, 24–31.

20. Ibid, 32–41.

21. André Gorz, *Ecology As Politics* (Boston: South End Press, 1980); Gorz, *Farewell to the Working Class* (Boston: South End Press, 1982); Gorz, *Paths to Paradise: On the Liberation from Work* (Boston: South End Press, 1985).

Notes for Chapter Two

1. Veronica Beechey and Tessa Perkins, *A Matter of Hours: Women, Part-Time Work and the Labour Market* (Minneapolis: University of Minnesota Press, 1987), 134.

2. Mary Frank Fox and Sharlene Hesse-Biber, *Women At Work* (Palo Alto, CA: Mayfield Publishing Company, 1984), 72–73.

3. Peter B. Doeringer and Michael J. Piore, *Internal Labor Market and Manpower Analysis* (Lexington: D.C. Heath, 1971).

4. Beechey and Perkins, 134.

5. Richard Edwards, *Contested Terrain: The Transformation of the Workplace in the Twentieth Century* (New York: Basic Books, 1979), 166.

6. Ibid., 165.

7. Randy Hodson and Teresa A. Sullivan, *The Social Organization of Work* (Belmont, CA: Wadsworth, 1990), appendix table 1.

8. Ibid.

9. Edwards, 167.

10. Hodson and Sullivan, appendix table 1.

11. Beechey and Perkins, 136.

12. For an examination of emotion work in the marketplace through the experience of flight attendants, see Arlie Russell Hochschild, *The Managed Heart: Commercialization of Human Feeling* (Berkeley: University of California Press, 1983).

13. Part-time professionals who receive prorated pay and benefits are exceptions to this. Some part-time professionals are negotiating for career-like progressions within the part-time track.

14. This bias against part-time employment is built into the conventional sociological definition of professions. In one standard text in the sociol-

ogy of work, the establishment of full-time occupations is delineated as one step in the process of the professionalization of occupations. See George Ritzer and David Walczak, *Working: Conflict and Change*, third edition (Englewood Cliffs, NJ: Prentice-Hall, 1986), 66.

15. Jonathan Grossman, "Fair Labor Standards Act of 1938: Maximum Struggle for a Minimum Wage," *Monthly Labor Review* (June 1978): 22.

16. Shirley J. Smith, "The Growing Diversity of Work Schedules," *Monthly Labor Review* 109 (November 1986): 7.

17. Ibid., 7.

18. Ibid., 7.

19. Ibid., 8–9.

20. Paul O. Flaim, "Work Schedules of Americans: An Overview of New Findings," *Monthly Labor Review* 109 (November 1986): 3.

21. Smith, 11.

22. Ibid., 12.

23. Earl F. Mellor, "Shift Work and Flexitime: How Prevalent Are They?" *Monthly Labor Review* 109 (November 1986): 18.

24. Flaim, 3.

25. Mellor, 14.

26. Flaim, 3.

27. The Federal Employees Flexible and Compressed Schedules Act of 1978 mandated implementation of flexitime throughout the federal civil service.

28. Mellor, 19.

29. Ibid., 19–20.

30. Steffan Linder, *The Harried Leisure Class* (New York: Columbia University Press, 1970), 12.

31. John P. Robinson, *How Americans Use Time* (New York: Praeger, 1977), 28.

32. Ibid., 29.

33. Ibid., 29, 35.

34. For a review of the literature on shiftwork and flexitime, see Graham L. Staines and Joseph H. Pleck, *The Impact of Work Schedules on the Family* (Ann Arbor, MI: Institute for Social Research, 1983), 20–29. For an analysis of

the adaptive work performed by shiftworkers' wives, see Rosanna Hertz and Joy Charlton, "Making Family Under a Shiftwork Schedule: Air Force Security Guards and Their Wives," *Social Problems* 36 (December 1989): 491–507.

35. Staines and Pleck, *The Impact of Work Schedules.*

36. Ibid., 2.

37. Ibid., 103.

38. Ibid., 3.

39. Sarah Fenstermaker Berk, *The Gender Factory: The Apportionment of Work in American Households* (New York: Plenum, 1985).

40. Ibid, 7.

41. Ibid, 8; K. E. Walker and M. Woods, *Time Use: A Measure of Household Production of Goods and Services* (Washington, DC: American Home Economics Association, 1976), 63.

42. Walker and Woods, *Time Use.*

43. Heidi Hartmann, "The Family as the Locus of Gender, Class, and Political Struggle: The Example of Housework." *Signs: Journal of Women in Culture and Society* 6 (Spring 1981): 383.

44. Ibid., 379.

45. Berk, 8.

46. Joseph H. Pleck, *Working Wives/Working Husbands* (Beverly Hills, CA: Sage Publications, 1985), 140.

47. Ibid., 141.

48. Ibid., 143.

49. Ibid., 146, 152.

50. Ibid., 152; specifically regarding the effects of household work-time on wages, see Shelley Coverman, "Gender, Domestic Labor Time, and Wage Inequality," *American Sociological Review* 48 (October 1983): 623–637.

51. Chloe E. Bird and Allen M. Fremont, "Gender, Time Use, and Health," *Journal of Health and Social Behavior* 32 (June 1991): 114–129. Specifically, the authors report that higher education, higher wages, and more hours of paid work improve health, whereas housework worsens it. Time in child care is not significantly related to health, and helping others has a positive effect on health among both women and men. They conclude that men accrue both economic and health advantages from their social roles as primary breadwinners—a conclusion that runs counter to the popular wisdom that

men's stressful occupations contribute to their higher rates of heart disease— and women would experience better health if gender roles were more equal.

52. Martin Meissner, "Sexual Division of Labour and Inequality: Labour and Leisure." In *Women in Canada*, ed., M. Stephenson (Toronto: The Women's Educational Press, 1977), cited in Berk, *The Gender Factory*, 9.

53. John P. Robinson, "Who's Doing the Housework?" *American Demographics* (December 1988), 26.

54. Pleck, 64, 72.

55. Ibid., 72.

56. Walker and Woods compare wives who are not employed to those employed 1 to 14 hours, 15 to 29 hours, and 30 or more hours per week. Applying the federal government's statistical definition of part-time employment, however, note that the last category lumps some part-time workers (30 to 34 hours per week) with full-time workers. Still, Walker and Woods draw finer distinctions among wives than husbands. Among husbands, they compare those employed less than 40 hours per week to those employed 40 to 49 hours or 50 hours or more. Pleck's analyses compare dual-earner and sole-breadwinner households without detailed attention to hours of employment.

57. Staines and Pleck, 109.

Notes for Chapter Three

1. C. Wright Mills, *The Sociological Imagination* (New York: Oxford University Press, 1959).

2. Brian Fay, *Critical Social Science* (Ithaca, NY: Cornell University Press, 1987), especially ch. 4.

3. Barney G. Glaser and Anselm L. Strauss, *The Discovery of Grounded Theory: Strategies for Qualitative Research* (New York: Aldine de Gruyter, 1967), 45–77; Anselm Strauss and Juliet Corbin, *Basics of Qualitative Research: Grounded Theory Procedures and Techniques* (Newbury Park, CA: Sage Publications, Inc., 1990), 176–193.

4. Glaser and Strauss, 62, 69.

5. U.S. Department of Labor, Bureau of Labor Statistics, *Employment and Wages, Annual Averages* (Washington, DC: Government Printing Office, 1986).

6. The Association for Management Success estimates that 16 percent of all companies in the Great Lakes region have some type of job sharing. In the midwest, 13 percent of companies accommodate some type of job sharing; in

the west, 8 percent; in the northeast, 7 percent; and in the south, 6 percent. A survey conducted in 1989 for the Conference Board revealed that 21 percent of a sample of 519 firms offered job-sharing programs, although the majority of these firms had only a handful of job-sharing teams. See Kathleen Christensen and Halina Maslanka, "Flexible Schedules in U.S. Businesses." In the Proceedings of the Second Annual Women's Policy Research Conference, Institute for Women's Policy Research, Washington, DC, 1–2 June 1990, pp. 201–207.

Notes for Chapter Four

1. U.S. Department of Labor, *Handbook of Labor Statistics* (Washington, DC: Government Printing Office, 1989), 10, 54.

2. William V. Deutermann, Jr. and Scott Campbell Brown, "Voluntary Part-Time Workers: A Growing Part of the Labor Force," *Monthly Labor Review* 101 (June 1978): 3–10.

3. Chris Tilly, "Reasons for the Continuing Growth of Part-Time Employment," *Monthly Labor Review* 114 (March 1991): 10–18.

4. U.S. Congress, Office of Technology Assessment, *Automation of America's Offices* (Washington, DC: Government Printing Office, 1985), 59–60.

5. 9 to 5, National Association of Working Women, *Working at the Margins: Part-Time and Temporary Workers in the U.S.* (Cleveland, OH: 9 to 5, National Association of WorkingWomen, 1986).

6. Susan McHenry and Linda Lee Small, "Does Part-Time Pay Off?" *Ms. Magazine* (March 1989): 88–94.

7. Joseph W. Duncan, "The Boom in Part-Timers," *Dun's Business Month* 122 (October 1983): 44.

8. Thomas Nardone, "Part-Time Workers: Who Are They?"*Monthly Labor Review* 109 (February 1986): 13–19.

9. Frank Swoboda, "New Concerns Arise Over Those Who Can Find Only Part-Time Jobs," *Louisville Courier-Journal*, 7 April 1991, E 2.

10. Ibid.

11. Ibid.

12. John D. Owen, "Why Part-Time Workers Tend To Be In Low-Wage Jobs," *Monthly Labor Review* 101 (June 1978): 11–14; Thomas Plewes, "Profile of the Part–Time Worker," in Association of Part-Time Professionals, *Part-Time Employmentin America: Highlights of the First National Conference on Part-Time Employment* (McLean, VA: Association of Part-Time Professionals, 1984), 1–20.

13. John Zalusky, "Presentation by John Zalusky," in Association of Part-Time Professionals, *Part-Time Employment in America: Highlights of the First National Conference on Part-Time Employment* (McLean, VA: Association of Part-Time Professionals, 1984), 32–34.

14. In retail trade today, even full-time workers' schedules can be bent to meet business needs. Many retail operations are open more than eight hours a day, five days a week. Full-time workers with forty-hour schedules can be scheduled to work eight hours a day, five days a week within a larger business week. Therefore, a full-time worker may work 10:00 AM to 7:00 PM one day and 12:00 M to 9:00 PM another day. That full-time worker also may not work all of his or her forty hours between Monday and Friday if the employer is open for business on Saturday and Sunday. In the supermarket industry where night, Sunday, and twenty-four-hour openings have become the norm, full-time workers may find themselves at work almost any hour of the day. We commonly associate shift work with workers in manufacturing industries and protective services, but shift work has also become increasingly common among full-time workers in retail trade.

15. The term "contingent work" was coined by Audrey Freedman, a labor economist at the Conference Board, to refer to part-time, temporary, and contract workers with no permanent ties to an employer. See William Serrin, "Part-Time Work New Labor Trend," *The New York Times*, 9 July 1986. Regarding the transformation of internal labor markets, see Eileen Appelbaum, "Restructuring Work: Temporary, Part-Time, and At-Home Employment," in *Computer Chips and Paper Clips: Technology and Women's Employment*, ed. Heidi I. Hartmann (Washington, DC: National Academy Press, 1987), 268–310.

16. James E. Long and Ethel B. Jones, "Part-Week Work by Married Women," *Southern Economic Journal* 46 (January 1980): 716–725; James E. Long and Ethel B. Jones, "Married Women in Part-Time Employment," *Industrial and Labor Relations Review* 34 (April 1981): 413–425; R. D. Morgenstern and W. Hamovitch, "Labor Supply of Married Women in Part-Time and Full-Time Occupations," *Industrial and Labor Relations Review* 30 (October 1976): 59–67; S. Yeandle, "Variation and Flexibility: Key Characteristics of Female Labor," *Sociology* 16 (August 1982): 422–430.

17. Their expectations of themselves as mothers, admittedly, may be the internalization of social standards and husband's expectations.

Notes for Chapter Five

1. Martin Gannon, "Preferences of Temporary Workers: Time Variety, Flexibility," *Monthly Labor Review* 107 (August 1984): 26–28.

2. T. R. Ostrach, "Second Look at Temporaries," *Personnel Journal* 60 (June 1981): 440.

3. Max L. Carey and Kim L. Hazelbaker, "Employment Growth in the Temporary Help Industry," *Monthly Labor Review* 109 (April 1986): 37–44.

4. Ostrach, "Second Look," 440.

5. U.S. Congress, Office of Technology Assessment, *Automation of America's Offices* (Washington, DC: Government Printing Office, 1985), 61.

6. Martin Gannon, "A Profile of the Temporary Help Industry and Its Workers," *Monthly Labor Review* 97 (May 1974): 44–49.

7. Martin Gannon, "Preferences of Temporary Workers: Time, Variety, Flexibility," *Monthly Labor Review* 107 (August 1984): 26–28.

8. Wayne J. Howe, "The Business Services Industry Sets Pace in Employment Growth," *Monthly Labor Review* 109 (April 1986): 29–36.

9. Gannon, "A Profile of the Temporary Help Industry."

10. Ibid.

11. Gannon, "Preferences of Temporary Workers," 28.

12. Virginia Olesen and Frances Katsuranis, "Urban Nomads: Women in Temporary Clerical Services," in *Women Working*, ed., Ann H. Stromberg and Shirley Harkess (Palo Alto, CA: Mayfield Publishing Company, 1978): 316–338.

13. Charles Horton Cooley, *Social Organization* (New York: Schocken, 1962).

14. Sara M. Evans, *Born for Liberty: A History of Women in America* (New York: The Free Press, 1989).

15. Volunteers are more likely to work for churches or other religious organizations than for any other kind of organization. Women are just slightly more likely than men to work for churches. Thirty-nine percent of female volunteers and 36 percent of male volunteers reported that working for churches was their main volunteer activity during the year ending in May 1989. See Howard V. Hayghe, "Volunteers in the U.S.: Who Donates the Time?" *Monthly Labor Review* 114 (February 1991): 21.

16. The two-person career occurs when a combination of formal and informal institutional demands is placed on both members of a married couple of whom only the man is employed by the institution. Usually, the wife is inducted into the orbit of her husband's employing institution not because of her own, or the institution's, specific choice but because she is related to her husband through sexual, economic, and emotional bonds. Her participation in his career is an extension of her role as wife. The typical, although by no means unique, two-person career is that of the corporate executive and his

wife. Her participation in his career, usually not acknowledged or remunerated directly, furthers his career by maintaining and perhaps, over the long
run, improving his status. See Hanna Papanek's classic statement, "Men,
Women, and Work: Reflections on the Two-Person Career," *American Journal
of Sociology* 78 (1973): 852–872.

Notes for Chapter Six

1. Barney Olmsted, "Job Sharing: An Emerging Workstyle," *International Labour Review* 118 (May–June 1979): 284.

2. Ibid., 283–297.

3. Gretl S. Meier, *Job Sharing: A New Pattern for Quality of Work and Life*
(Kalamazoo, MI: W. E. Upjohn Institute for Employment Research, 1979);
Kathleen Christensen and Halina Maslanka, "Flexible Schedules in U.S. Businesses." In the *Proceedings of the Second Annual Women's Policy Research Conference*, Institute for Women's Policy Research, Washington, DC, 1–2 June 1990,
pp. 201–207.

4. Meier, xi.

5. Ibid.

6. Cynthia Negrey, "Job Sharing, Contingent Autonomy, and Labor
Control." In the *Proceedings of the Second Annual Women's Policy Research Conference*, Institute for Women's Policy Research, Washington, DC, 1–2 June 1990,
pp. 208–213.

7. Carmen Sirianni, "Self-Management of Time: A Democratic Alternative," *Socialist Review* 88/4 (1988): 36.

8. Beverly H. Burris, "Employed Mothers: The Impact of Class and
Marital Status on the Prioritizing of Family and Work," *Social Science Quarterly*
72 (March 1991): 50–66.

9. Rosemary Deem, *All Work and No Play? A Study of Women and
Leisure* (Milton Keynes, England and Philadelphia: Open University Press,
1986).

10. Technically, "Americans" refers to the civilian non-institutionalized
population sixteen years old and over. These findings are based on data from
the May 1989 Current Population Survey as reported by Howard V. Hayghe
in "Volunteers in the U.S.: Who Donates the Time?" *Monthly Labor Review* 114
(February 1991): 17–23.

Notes for Chapter Seven

1. Fred Best, *Flexible Life Scheduling: Breaking the Education-Work-Retirement Lockstep* (New York: Praeger, 1980).

2. Ibid, 84. Also Fred Best, *Work Sharing: Issues, Policy Options, and Prospects* (Kalamazoo, MI: W. E. Upjohn Institute for Employment Research, 1981), 2.

3. Alfred Blumrosen and Ruth Gerber Blumrosen, "The Duty to Plan for Fair Employment Revisited: Work Sharing in Hard Times," *Rutgers Law Review* 28 (Summer): 1082–1106.

4. Best, *Flexible Life Scheduling*, 85.

5. Kim Watford, "Shorter Workweeks: An Alternative to Layoffs," *Business Week*, 14 April 1986, 77–78.

6. Robert W. Bednarzik, "Worksharing in the U.S.: Its Prevalence and Duration," *Monthly Labor Review* 103 (July 1980): 3–12.

7. Best, *Work Sharing*; Ramelle MaCoy and Martin J. Morand, *Short-Time Compensation: A Formula for Work Sharing* (New York: Pergamon Press, 1984); Maureen McCarthy and Gail S. Rosenberg with Gary Lefkowitz, *Work Sharing: Case Studies* (Kalamazoo, MI: W. E. Upjohn Institute for Employment Research, 1981).

8. Sometimes two coworkers "double up," each taking a turn doing both jobs, thereby creating extra free time on the job. See Ben Hamper, *Rivethead: Tales from the Assembly Line* (New York: Warner Books, 1991).

9. Under technical systems of labor control, machines, such as the assembly line, set the pace of work, and workers must adjust their work rhythms to the machines. For a detailed discussion of technical systems of labor control see Richard Edwards, *Contested Terrain: The Transformation of the Workplace in the Twentieth Century* (New York: Basic Books, 1979).

Notes for Chapter Eight

1. André Gorz, *Farewell to the Working Class* (Boston: South End Press, 1982).

2. André Gorz, *Paths to Paradise: On the Liberation from Work* (Boston: South End Press, 1985).

3. Gorz, *Farewell*, 72.

4. Ibid., 71.

5. Ibid., 73.

6. Ibid., 114–115, 137.

7. U.S. Congress, House of Representatives, Committee on Education and Labor, *To Revise the Overtime Compensation Requirements of the Fair Labor Standards Act of 1938*, Hearings before the Subcommittee on Labor Standards, 96th Congress, 1st Session, on H.R. 1784, October 23–25 (Washington, DC: Government Printing Office, 1979).

8. William McGaughey, Jr., *A Shorter Workweek in the 1980s* (White Bear Lake, MN: Thistlerose Publications, 1981), 109.

9. Ibid., 256. For further discussion of the pros and cons of work-time reduction see Rolande Cuvillier, *The Reduction of Working Time* (Geneva: International Labour Office, 1984); Ronald G. Ehrenberg and Paul L. Schumann, *Longer Hours or More Jobs? An Investigation of Amending Hours Legislation to Create Employment* (Ithaca, New York: New York State School of Industrial and Labor Relations, Cornell University, 1982); and McGaughey, *A Shorter Workweek*.

10. For arguments in support of a "mommy track," see Felice Schwartz, "Management Women and the New Facts of Life," *Harvard Business Review* (January–February, 1989): 65–75. Barbara Ehrenreich and Deidre English offer an excellent critique of Schwartz' proposals in "Blowing the Whistle on the 'Mommy Track'," *Ms. Magazine* 18 (July–August, 1989): 56–58.

11. For a discussion of the cult of domesticity, see Nancy F. Cott, *The Bonds of Womanhood* (New Haven: Yale University Press, 1977) and Julie A. Matthaei, *An Economic History of Women in America* (New York: Schocken Books, 1982).

12. The power of capital to resist reductions in working time, however, is reflected in the trend today to extend the hours during which children are at school. I am referring especially to the growth of before and after-school care provided by some school systems (at cost to parents) particularly in affluent areas. There has also been some discussion of extending the school year through the summer. These trends suggest it is the public schools that will be the providers of substitute child care for working parents.

13. Robert N. Bellah, Richard Madsen, William M. Sullivan, Ann Swidler, and Steven M. Tipton, *Habits of the Heart: Individualism and Commitment in American Life* (New York: Perennial Library/Harper and Row, 1985).

14. The operative definition of political participation here is that of participation in formal political activities. This is not to deny that politics exist at the interpersonal level in everyday life and, therefore, are pervasive. Further, if recent rates of voter turnout are any indication, the majority of American citizens are politically alienated. A recent Census Bureau report indicates that

both registration and voter turnout dropped in 1990 compared to 1986, non-presidential election years. Forty-five percent of eligible adults voted in the 1990 midterm elections compared with 46 percent in 1986. Voter registration declined from 64 percent of eligible adults to 62 percent. See "Fewer People in U.S. Turning Out to Vote," *Louisville Courier-Journal*, 29 November 1991, B 5. Even smaller proportions participate in political organizations. A recent survey indicates that about 20 percent of Americans do volunteer work and 13 percent of all volunteers work for political and civic organizations. See Howard V. Hayghe, "Volunteers in the U.S.: Who Donates the Time?" Monthly Labor Review 114 (February 1991): 17, 21.

15. Alan Wolfe, "New Directions in the Marxist Theory of Politics," *Politics and Society* 4 (1974): 131–159.

16. Sara M. Evans and Harry C. Boyte, *Free Spaces: The Sources of Democratic Change in America* (New York: Harper and Row).

17. Carmen Sirianni, "Economies of Time in Social Theory: Three Approaches Compared," *Current Perspectives in Social Theory* 8: 184.

18. Robert B. Reich, *The Next American Frontier* (New York: Times Books, 1983).

19. Pamela Adelmann, "Freshening Freud For Us All," *Detroit Free Press*, 13 September 1987.

20. For a critical discussion of therapy in modern American society, see Bellah et al., *Habits of the Heart*. They argue that therapy takes for granted the institutions and organizations of advanced industrial society and "helps" individuals maneuver within those institutions. Despite its orientation to encouraging the development of autonomous persons, it is blind to the ways in which social institutions circumscribe autonomy. Because of this myopia, therapy rarely encourages individuals to join together to change social institutions.

21. Sigmund Freud, *Civilization and Its Discontents* (New York: W. W. Norton and Co., Inc., 1961).

Index

DATE DUE